WAIT FOR ME AT THE BOTTOM OF THE POOL

The Writings of Jack Smith
Edited by J. Hoberman and Edward Leffingwell

SERPENT'S TAIL

HIGH RISK
BOOKS
in collaboration with
ICA/P.S.1

NEW YORK / LONDON

CINEMAROC NICELODEON
presents~
Jack Smith's

Wait For Me at the

Bottom of the Pool

A Lobster Moon
Mixed Media Spectacle
On Roof of building at 89 Grand St.
Fri. and Sat. Oct 18 and 19 at 8:30 pm

See! Mario Montez
in slides of Burning Beauty!!
Hear! Glamercials of Barblonjet!!!!!
See! All the Splendours that were Atlantis!

Acknowledgements

The editors wish to thank Penny Arcade, Richard Bellamy, Ira Cohen, Dianne Conley, Diane di Prima, Mary D. Dorman, David Gurin, Marvin Heiferman, Ken Jacobs, Kathe Izzo, Carole Kismaric, Jonas Mekas, Ira Silverberg, Alanna Stang, and Hiro Yamagata for their generous assistance. This collection was developed in collaboration with the Institute for Contemporary Art: P.S. 1 on behalf of which Alanna Heiss, Mark Leyer, Patrick Pardo, Dennis Szakacs, and Tony Vasconcellos gave unstinting support. Lisa Bateman deserves a special measure of gratitude for her considerable contribution to the preservation, transcription, and organization of the anthologized material.

Contents

Capitalism of Lotusland

Could art be useful? Ever since the desert glitter drifted over the burnt-out ruins of Plaster Lagoon thousands of artists have pondered and dreamed of such a thing, yet, art must not be used anymore as another elaborate means of fleeing from thinking because of the multiplying amount of information each person needs to process in order to come to any kind of decision about what kind of planet one wants to live on before business, religion, and government succeed in blowing it out of the solar system.

Let art continue to be entertaining, escapist, stunning, glamorous, and NATURALISTIC – but let it also be loaded with information worked into the vapid plots of, for instance, movies. Each one would be a more or less complete exposition of one subject or another. Thus you would have Tony Curtis and Janet Leigh busily making yogurt; Humphrey Bogart struggling to introduce a basic civil law course into public schools; infants being given to the old in homes for the aged by Ginger Rogers; donut-shaped dwellings with sunlight pouring into central patios for all, designed by Gary Cooper; soft, clear plastic bubble cars with hooks that attach to monorails built by Charlton Heston that pass over the Free Paradise of abandoned objects in the center of the city near where the community movie sets would also be; and where Maria Montez and Johnny Weismüller would labour to dissolve all national boundaries and release the prisoners of Uranus. But the stairway to socialism is blocked up by the Yvonne de Carlo Tabernacle Choir waving bloody palm branches and waiting to sing the "Hymn to the Sun" by Irving Berlin. This is the rented moment of EXOTIC LANDLORDISM OF PREHISTORIC CAPITALISM OF TABU.

LAICA Journal #19 (June/July 1978)

The text derives from a longhand performance manuscript for *"Irrational Landlordism of Bagdad,"* presented on the occasion of the Cologne Art Fair, 1977. The original Cologne text is intended as a taped voiceover accompanying a scene featuring a woman scrubbing floors in a factory room. At the conclusion of the narration, the scrub lady rises, a glamorous forelady enters, the scrub lady sinks to her knees again, crushed, and resumes mopping. The forelady inspects, "glad to be earlier than usual." (E.L.)

In a November 1978 interview with the coeditor, Smith referred to this oft-cited manifesto as "the best single chunk of writing I ever made." (J.H.)

JACK SMITH: BAGDADA AND LOBSTERREALISM

By J. Hoberman

People never know why they do what they do. But they have to have explanations for themselves and others.

– JACK SMITH, "BELATED APPRECIATION OF V.S." (1963)

There was, in the early 1960s, at more or less the time when television had saturated the American market, a sense that movies – and not just individual movies but The Movies – were a form of culture, even *the* form of American culture. "At this moment in movie history," wrote Jack Smith in the Winter 1962/63 issue of a journal itself called *Film Culture*, "there is an enveloping cloud of critical happiness – it's OK to love movies now."

More than Okay: *Film Culture*'s madly eclectic Winter 1962/63 issue offered an impressive panoply of cinephilic position papers: Andrew Sarris's studious "Notes on the Auteur Theory in 1962" was followed by Manny Farber's more rambunctious attack on high culture, "White Elephant Art Vs. Termite Art." Pauline Kael's appreciation of Francois Truffaut's nouvelle vague *Shoot the Piano Player* segued into Gregory Markopoulos's celebration of fellow-filmmaker Ron Rice's underground travelogue, *Senseless*. There was a lengthy Q & A with experimental animator Robert Breer (pictured on the journal's cover) while the veteran left-wing film historian Seymour Stern, having fired his previous interlocutor, interviewed himself. But nothing included in that remarkable issue was more radical than Jack Smith's "The Perfect Filmic Appositeness of Maria Montez."

Jack Smith was to shortly startle the world with *Flaming Creatures*, the underground movie he'd shot during the summer of 1962 and was even then editing (and was, in a sense, explaining with this essay), but his name was still unknown. Indeed, those who first read "The Perfect Film Appositeness of Maria Montez" might well have imagined the author to be using a pseudonym – so outrageous was his premise. Courting ridicule,

Smith opened the door on a "whole gaudy array of secret-flix." In a beat, telegraphic prose style, he proposed a personal canon of genre films from the '30s and '40s. These secret flix, all from the period of his childhood and adolescence, tended towards the tropical and excessive; "Spanish Galleon flix," Caribbean horror movies like *White Zombie*, "Dorothy Lamour sarong flix," movies featuring Bela Lugosi and the hillbilly come- dienne Judy Canova, Busby Berkeley extravaganzas, and all musicals with production numbers set in Rio de Janeiro. [1]

Sarris and Farber practiced a relatively discreet form of Hollywood con- noisseurship. Smith's bias was proudly a-literate. ("Do you ever worry about a particular subtlety in your films not being understood?" Gerard Malanga would ask him in a 1967 interview. "How can you not – you know – understand the movements and the gestures?" was Smith's reply. "The appeal is not to the understanding, anyway.") On one hand, "The Perfect Film Appositeness of Maria Montez" downgraded narrative to insist upon the essentially visual nature of movies. On the other, as its title made clear, the essay was consecrated to the mystery of the human presence. Smith argued that the acme of cinematic expressiveness was to be found in a series of juvenile-adventure films produced at Universal Studios during World War II as vehicles for a Dominican-born actress who, by conventional standards, could barely be said to be acting at all.

Daughter of a Spanish diplomat and a Dutch refugee, Smith's lifelong muse grew up in the Dominican Republic, acted as a teenager in Europe, modeled briefly in New York, and, in 1940, landed a contract with Universal more on the basis of her exotic beauty and flamboyant self-pro- motion than any discernible acting talent. Cast by producer Walter Wanger as Scheherazade in Universal's first Technicolor production *Arabian Nights* (1942), Maria Montez enjoyed considerable, if brief, popu- larity in a series of follow-up vehicles, including *White Savage* (1943), *Ali Baba and the 40 Thieves*, *Cobra Woman*, *Gypsy Wildcat* (all 1944), and *Sudan* (1945). Then the Montez career faltered. The temperamental star was relegated to black and white, replaced by Universal's "Queen of Technicolor," Yvonne De Carlo. After starring in the independent *Siren of*

Atlantis (1949), Montez left Hollywood for Europe where she appeared in several French and Italian productions, some with her husband Jean-Pierre Aumont. On September 7, 1951, she suffered a fatal heart attack while taking her daily reducing bath.

According to playwright Ronald Tavel, another Montez partisan who first encountered Smith in the intellectual Casbah that was the early '60s Lower East Side, Smith had been working as an usher at the Orpheum Theater in Chicago in 1951 when the publicity caused by Montez's untimely death inspired the management to undertake an extended festival of her wartime films. "It was then and there," Tavel would write, that the 19-year-old Smith "became familiar with the star whom he has since referred to as The Wonderful One or The Marvelous One. He felt that all the secrets of the cinema lay in careful study of the woman..."

***

Having Maria Montez as a favorite star has not been gratuitous (tho it was in 1945) since it has left a residue of notions, interesting to me as a film-maker and general film aesthete.

– Jack Smith, "The Perfect Cinematic Appositeness of Maria Montez" (1962)

I remember a Jack Smith slide show in the early 1970s at which a well-known and influential pair of film academics ostentatiously flounced out of the theater, somewhere in the West Village, apparently unable to endure the extended, dreamy barrage of green-tinted, black-and-white Montez publicity stills which the artist projected as slides accompanied by a schlocky instrumental version of Leonard Bernstein's "Maria." [2]

More than a fetish or a cult figure, Maria Montez provided Smith with an entire worldview. *Buzzards Over Bagdad*, his first (and unfinished) movie, takes its title (one he recycled several times) from a particular image in *Arabian Nights* – the same movie that provides the first four minutes of the *Flaming Creatures* sound track. Smith's subsequent films and theater pieces are rife with specific references to Montez movies. *What's*

Underground About Marshmallows? (the 1981 performance monologue which later formed the basis for Ron Vawter's 1992 one-man theater-piece *Roy Cohn/Jack Smith*) includes a ritual recitation of the Montez filmography. Most of the *Normal Love* interiors are shot around the Montez shrine constructed in the midst of a 14th Street apartment and tended by Smith's greatest superstar, Maria Montez, while Smith's journals attest that, for him, Montez veneration was more than "almost like praying."

The notion of Maria Montez as cinema goddess was campy to be sure – although Smith's *Film Culture* paean appeared two years before Susan Sontag would publish her "Notes on Camp" in the Fall 1964 issue of *Partisan Review* (and a good fifteen years before *Film Comment* instituted a regular feature asking famous movie personalities to list their celluloid "guilty pleasures"). In any case, just as Maria Montez ranked far below Maria Callas (for example) on the diva scale, so most of the secret-flix Smith celebrated in "The Perfect Film Appositeness of Maria Montez" were considerably more outre than those Sontag would cite. [3]

If these movies were junk, Smith never denied it: "Trash," he proclaimed, "is the material of creators." Secret-flix cannot be remade but only exhumed. "The Memoirs of Maria Montez," first published in *Film Culture* in the heady aftermath of *Flaming Creatures*'s spring 1963 release, suggests – no less than Smith's chef d'oeuvre – a ritual set in a derelict movie studio. (In this case, the star is a decomposing corpse.) The trash heap is a recurring Smith trope. A collector of cultural detritus, a connoisseur of "moldiness," he was an aesthete with an acute sense of collapse and failure. In his oft-cited manifesto "Capitalism of Lotusland," a section of the 1977 performance-piece *Irrational Landlordism of Bagdad*, Smith refers to a Free Paradise of abandoned objects (located, significantly, near the community movie sets). In the 1978 *Semiotext(e)* interview which illuminates the second half of his career as "The Perfect Film Appositeness of Maria Montez" does the first, Smith envisions a city organized around a giant junkyard. "I think this center of unused objects and unwanted objects would become a center of intellectual activity. Things would grow up around it."

Flaming Creatures may have afforded Smith a youthful *succes de scandal* but, for the most part, his was a marginal existence lived on the edge of bohemian squalor. "A man of imagination suffering pre-fashionable Lower East Side deprivation and consumed with American 1950's, '40's, and '30's disgust" was how filmmaker Ken Jacobs described the subject of his pre-1962 Smith portrait *Blonde Cobra*. ("Playing hide-and-seek with odors" is Smith's phrase in *What's Underground About Marshmallows?*) Smith was a legendary character, the Alfred Jarry of the East Village. Tall and skinny, he didn't look or sound or act or talk like anyone else. His distinctive, high-pitched drawl (filled with hesitations, yet precise in its diction; fun to imitate, perfect for expressing feigned confusion) managed to evoke somnolence and hysteria in equal measure.

Smith's vocabulary was equally singular. "Exotic," of course, was the supreme compliment. "Moldy" referred to the dated artifacts of the recent past. "Pasty," an adjective synonymous with false or phony, was not necessarily pejorative – although the Smithism "pasty normal" was a dismissive term for heterosexual. "Goosy" (derived from gossamer) was the sort of elegant costume one might wear to appear in an art deco movie. "Superstar," Smith's most famous coinage, was appropriated by Andy Warhol – Andy Panda in the Jack Smith bestiary, which also include "creatures" (everyone), "mynah birds" (imitators), the Penguin (a sort of sympathetic costar alterego), and the Lobster (epitome of the avaricious landlord) who increasingly held the world in his grip.

Casting himself as "Donald Flamingo, just a local personality trying to make a living" or (perhaps more bitterly in his reference to *What Makes Sammy Run?*) as "Sinbad Glick," Smith lived in the gap between exotic fantasy and ordinary reality. Film, as he writes in "The Perfect Film Appositeness of Maria Montez," is not a strip of celluloid but a place "where it is possible to clown, to pose, to act out fantasies, to not be seen while one gives." In the late 1960s, thanks to his patron Isabel Eberstadt, Smith occupied the two top floors of a loft building on the corner of Grand and Greene Streets in the Lower Manhattan cast-iron district not yet known as Soho. "I'm recreating Bagdad," he told Ronald

Tavel, having knocked out the greater portion of the floor separating the two spaces and thus created the mound of plaster which would provide the stage set for his theatricals.

Of course, as Tavel would disapprovingly note, Smith had no interest in the real Bagdad. His obsession was, rather, with what Parker Tyler, in his Surrealist-inflected film criticism, had called the Hollywood Hallucination – or, rather, with the memory of that hallucination. In part, Smith's appreciation for Montez movies was a Surrealist taste. ("Learn to go see the 'worst' films: they are sometimes sublime," Ado Kyrou advised in *Le Surréalism au Cinéma*, first published in 1963). Montez vehicles like *White Savage*, *Ali Baba and the Forty Thieves*, and *Cobra Woman* are founts of inane, voluptuously exotic imagery. Smith was moved by their poetry – and, as the Surrealists strove to fuse their waking existence with dreams, so he wished to imbue ordinary life with the splendor he recognized in Montezland. [4]

"At least in America a Maria Montez could believe she was the Cobra Woman, the Siren of Atlantis, Scheherezade, etc.," is how Smith began his paean to Montez.

> She believed and thereby made the people who went to
> her movies believe. Those who could believe, did.
> Those who saw the World's Worst Actress just couldn't
> and they missed the magic. Too bad – their loss . . .

It was precisely because Montez was so unconvincing an actress that Smith valued her performances. "One of her atrocious acting sighs suffused a thousand tons of dead plaster with imaginative life and a truth." The truth was that Montez was always herself – her films were unintended documentaries of a romantic, narcissistic young woman dressing up in pasty jewels, striking fantastic poses, queening it over an obvious make-believe world. For Smith, these inept portrayals hyperbolized the actual situation of a Hollywood glamour goddess. "A bad actor is rich, unique, idiosyncratic, revealing." [5]

Montez's transparent role-playing, and her unconcealed delight at being the center of attention, were more authentic to Smith than the naturalism achieved by *successfully* phony actresses. Yvonne De Carlo, by contrast, was, as Montez's scheming successor, the personification of the soulless and ersatz, what he would later call "a walking career." For Smith, sympathetic to Mary Baker Eddy and the mind-over-matter dogma of Christian Science, acting transformed not the actor, but the world. Montez's films were created less by Hollywood than by the force of the actress's lunatic conviction:

> The vast machinery of a movie company worked overtime
> to make her visions into sets. They achieved only
> inept approximations.

It was in the realm of Inept Approximation that Smith's productions, from *Flaming Creatures* through *The Secret of Rented Island* to the 1984 piece whose taped transcription is labeled "Penguin Panic in the Rented Desert," derived their pathos, their purity, and their grandeur.

***

I realize that finishing a film for me is not a matter of years but decades.
– JACK SMITH, GRANT APPLICATION (9/14/82)

Jack Smith's writings include a legacy of critical appreciations, journal entries, scenarios, stories, memoirs, performance scripts, and transcribed lectures. Most of those that were published appeared in the early '60s: "I didn't get any encouragement, no reception for the writing, so I just stopped," Smith told Gerard Malanga.

Ranging from ecstatic aesthetic manifestos to scabrous gross-out comedies of sexual disgust ("her flaccid, grayish white anus collapsed with a crash to the scrawny Arab man's black horsecock of pleasure"), Smith's writings are at once unclassifiable and all of a piece – the autodidactic autobiography of a particular sensibility. In his first published essays,

"The Perfect Film Appositeness of Maria Montez" and "Belated Appreciation of V.S.," he provided the two best explications which *Flaming Creatures* would ever have – even predicting his and the film's fate. Montez vehicles were chopped up on TV, "cut & stabbed & punished. All are now safe from Montez embarrassment." Sternberg went too far in his obsessions and "was punished . . . ostensibly because he had violated good technique."

Smith certainly violated good taste as well as good technique: "The more rules broken the more enriched becomes the activity," he maintained. Given the success and notoriety of *Flaming Creatures*, which had its theatrical premiere in April 1963 and was confiscated by the New York Police Department and banned by the state a bit more than ten months later, he was more or less compelled to ponder the libidinal economy of the movies. His journal entries include a powerful and poignant defense of pornography (as well, at least by inference, of Hollywood). "Sexual fantasizing is the pitiful means whereby the truly unpleasant difficult sex function is swathed in glamour, perversity, and ultimately, simply, interest."

Similarly, Smith needed enemies against which to define himself. (The subject of *Blonde Cobra*, Ken Jacobs wrote, "knows that a state of indignity can serve to show his character in sharpest relief.") Smith's 1965 performance piece, *Rehearsal for the Destruction of Atlantis,* grew out of the pot bust, protest, and subsequent arrest he describes in the journal entry titled "Lobotomy in Lobsterland." Ultimately, it would be the filmmaker/writer/archivist Jonas Mekas who became the focal point for Smith's rage. Originally Smith's producer, distributor, exhibitor, publicist, publisher, and general benefactor, Mekas embodied the mirage of early fame. By the early '70s – when Smith felt himself living in the debased De Carlo movie he called the "Rented World" – Mekas had evolved into a figure variously referred to as "Uncle Fishook," "Uncle Roachcrust," and "Uncle Pawnshop," the keeper of the Mausoleum (Anthology Film Archives) who had trapped Smith, among other "sugar zombies," in the marshmallow illusion of promised success. *I Was a Mekas Collaborator* and

I Was a Male Yvonne De Carlo for the Lucky Landlord Underground were the mock confessional titles Smith gave to two late performance pieces.

In lieu of the movies, Smith created his own place. As late as "Penguin Panic in the Rented Desert" – after the official death of his stuffed animal co-star "Yolanda La Pinguina" and the retirement of "Donald Flamingo" to an "Aloha Community" of plastic palm trees – Smith was still refining his Maria Montez scenario. Digressing on the subject of orange juice ("It's so much like drinking . . . lobster blood"), in the midst of a drama of Hollywood studio intrigue, Smith (here Sinbad Glick) contemplates the mechanism at hand. The juicer is shaped like Aladdin's lamp: "It comes to a Bagdadian point!"

There can be no higher or more heartfelt complement. Applied to an audience, "the scum of Bagdad" was Jack Smith's term of approval. It was, of course, a privilege to have been a member of that crowd.

1. For the New York City art world, Fall 1962 had been the season of Pop. The so-called New Realism show that brought together Jim Dine, Robert Indiana, Roy Lichtenstein, Claes Oldenburg, James Rosenquist, George Segal, Andy Warhol, and Tom Wesselman opened at the Sidney Janis gallery on Halloween. (The following week, Warhol exhibited his Marilyn Monroe and Campbell Soup silkscreens at the Stable gallery.) On December 13, the Museum of Modern Art held a contentious symposium on the newly-emerged and named "Pop" Art. Was "The Perfect Film Appositeness of Maria Montez" then a Pop Art prank along the lines of Warhol's "Red Elvis"?

2. Carol Rowe offers another interpretation of this event in the introduction to his published dissertation *The Baudelairean Cinema: A Trend within the American Avant-Garde* (UMI Research Press, 1982). If any members of the audience were forcibly ejected by the irate artist, however, this spectator was blissfully unaware of it.

3. At the end of his entry on Robert Siodmak in *The American Cinema*, Andrew Sarris notes that, among other things, Siodmak directed "Maria Montez at her most deliriously defective in a dual role for *Cobra Woman*" – adding that, "without Maria Montez we might have been spared Jack Smith's

Flaming Creatures." (Sarris is careful to absolve his own particular fetish-object: "Siodmak is not to blame for spawning those mutants of the medium, the moviepoids.")

From another part of the aesthetic spectrum, the Warhol superstar Ondine published a "Letter to an Unknown Woman Namely Jack Smith" in the Summer 1967 issue of *Film Culture*, attacking the cult around "a minor film star of the 40's whose films' only value lie in the fact of its complete lack of standards." A postscript to the diatribe advises Montez's fans to worship rather a star who can be identified by her first name: "Maria . . . Maria who? Ouspensakia . . . Maria Schell, who? Who do you mean?"

4. Montez inspired even the most prosaic to surrealist flights. According to *The Saturday Evening Post*'s Hollywood correspondent Pete Martin, "writing about Montez is the next best thing to being allowed to jot down anything that jumps into your head" (*Hollywood Without Makeup*, 1948).

5. Acting, for Smith, was the triumphant presentation of self. "Another secret of acting is in your uh . . . most dramatic moments you contrive to be peeling onions," he advises wouldbe performers in *What's Underground About Marshmallows?* Thinking on stage was interesting, whereas "memorized speech (was) possibly the least dramatic thing that can happen on the stage or anywhere." The movies taught him the rich emotional power (and revelation) of the phony. Tavel recalls Smith's interest in Lynn Bari, a Caucasian actress cast as an Asian villainess in a number of 1930s Charlie Chan and Mr. Moto thrillers.

THE PERFECT FILMIC APPOSITENESS
OF MARIA MONTEZ

"In Paris I can do no wrong, they love me there."
– Maria Montez

a few years later: "Elle ne desert pas le nom d'actrice."
– A Paris paper reviewing a film she made there.

At least in America a Maria Montez could believe she was the Cobra woman, the Siren of Atlantis, Scheherazade, etc. She believed and thereby made the people who went to her movies believe. Those who could believe, did. Those who saw the World's Worst Actress just couldn't and they missed the magic. Too bad – their loss. Their magic comes from the most inevitable execution of the conventional pattern of acting. What they can appreciate is what most people agree upon – GOOD PERFS. Therefore you can have GOOD PERFS & no real belief. GOOD PERFS that give you no magic – oh I guess a sort of magic, a magic of sustained efficient operation (like the wonder that the car motor held out so well after a long trip).

But I tell you Maria Montez Moldy Movie Queen, Shoulder pad, gold platform wedgie Siren, Determined, dreambound, Spanish, Irish, Negro?, Indian girl who went to Hollywood from the Dominican Rep. Wretch actress – pathetic as actress, why insist upon her being an actress – why limit her? Don't slander her beautiful womanliness that took joy in her own beauty and all beauty – or whatever in her that turned plaster cornball sets to beauty. Her eye saw not just beauty but incredible, delirious, drug-like hallucinatory beauty.

The vast machinery of a movie company worked overtime to make her vision into sets. They achieved only inept approximations. But one of her atrocious acting sighs suffused a thousand tons of dead plaster with imaginative life and truth.

Woman and yet imaginator / believer / child / simple pathetically believing with no defenses – a beautiful woman who could fantasy – do you know of a woman like that? There aren't any. Never before, never since – this was an extraordinary unique person. Women – people – don't come in combinations that can/can't happen again:

fantasy - beauty

child - siren

creature - straight etc. because each is all these plus its opposite – and to dig one woman is to mysteriously evoke all others and not from watching actresses give PERFS does one feel anything real about woman, about films, about the world, various as it is for all of us, about men. But to see one person – OK if only by some weird accident – exposing herself – having fun, believing in moldiness (still moldy, but if it can be true for her and produces delight – the delight of technicolor movies – then it would be wonderful if it could be true for us).

And in a crazy way it is all true for us because she is one of us. Is it invalid of her to be the way she is? If so, none of us are valid – a position each one of us feels a violation of oneself if taken by another person (whatever our private thoughts may be). If you think you are invalid you may be the person who ridicules Montez movies. To admit of Maria Montez validities would be to turn on to moldiness, Glamorous Rapture, schizophrenic delight, hopeless naivete, and glittering technicolored trash!

"Geef me that Coparah chewel!"
"Geef me that Coparah chewel!"
– line of dialogue from Cobra Woman, *possibly the greatest line of dialogue in any American flic.*
"Juvenile . . . trash . . ."
– Jesse Zunser, N.Y. reviewer.

Juvenile does not equal shameful and trash is the material of creators. It exists whether one approves or not. You may not approve of the Orient but it's half of the world and it's where spaghetti came from. Trash *is* true of Maria Montez flix but so are jewels, Cobra jewels and so is wondrous refinement –

Night – the villain / high priest enters the bedroom of the old queen (good) and stabs her in her bed. Seen thru a carved screen in bkgrnd – at that moment – the sacred volcano erupts (orange light flashes) Old queen stares balefully (says something?) and dies. Now the cobra priestess (the evil sister) and the high priest can seize Jon Hall betrothed to / and the good sister (rightful ruler) and imprison them with no opposition. Persecution of Cobra Island – Crushing offerings demanded for King Cobra –
(Chunk of scenario synopsized)

There is a (unsophisticated, certainly) validity there – also theatrical drama (the best kind) – also interesting symbolism, delirious hokey, glamour – unattainable (because once possessed) and juvenile at its most passionate.

If you scorn Montez-land (now gone anyway so you are safe from its con-tamination) you are safely out of something you were involved in once and you resent (in direct ratio to your scorn, even to rage) not being able to go back – resent the closed, rainbow colored gates, resent not being wanted there, being a drag on the industry.

Well, it's gone with the war years (when you know that your flic is going to make money you indulge in hokey – at these times when investments must be certain you must strictly follow banker-logic), Universal probably demolished the permanent Montez-land sets. Vera West committed sui-cide in her blackmail swimming pool.[1] Montez dead in her bathtub from too much reducing salts. The colors are faded. Reel-Art Co. sold all her flix to T.V.

Montez-land (created of one woman's belief – not an actress') was made manifest on this earth, changed the world – 15 to 20 flix they made around her – OK – vehicles (the idea of vehicles shouldn't be condemned because it has been abused), vehicles that were medium for her belief therefore necessary, a justice, a need felt – Real – as investment, as lots of work for extras, hilarious to serious persons, beloved to Puerto-Ricans, magic for me, beauty for many, a camp to homos, Fauve American unconsciousness to Europeans etc.

Can't happen again. Fantasies now feature weight lifters who think now how lucky and clever they were to get into the movies & the fabulous pay . . . , think something like that on camera – it's contagious & you share those thots (which is a magical fantasy too but another article on "The Industry"). All are now safe from Maria Montez outrages! I suppose the color prints are destroyed now. Still, up until about 5 yrs. ago (when they were bought up by T.V.), Montez reissues cropped up at tiny nabes – every week one or another of them played somewhere in N.Y.C. At that time they were 12 to 17 years old. When they are shown now on T.V. they are badly chopped up, with large chunks missing. The pattern being repeated – their irresistibility resulting in their being cut & stabbed & punished. All are now safe from Montez embarrassment – the tiny nabes are torn down, didn't even make supermarkets – the big nabes have to get back investments so can't be asked (who'd ask) to show them. The art houses are committed to seriousness and importance, essays on celluloid (once it was sermons on celluloid), food for thought imported from THE CONTINENT. No more scoldings from critics . . .

At this moment in movie history there is a feeling of movies being approved of. There is an enveloping cloud of critical happiness – it's OK to love movies now. General approval (nobody knowing who starts it – but it's OK for you and everybody else). It's a pretty diffuse and general thing. Maria Montez flix were particular – you went for your particular reasons – had specific feelings from them & about them. It was a peculiarly idiosyncratic experience and heartily despised by critics. Critics are writers. They like writing – and written characters. Maria Montez's appeal was on a purely intuitive level. She was the bane of critics – that person whose effect cannot be known by words, described in words, flaunts words (her *image* spoke). Film critics are writers and they are hostile and uneasy in the presence of a visual phenomenon. They are most delighted by bare images that through visual barrenness call thought into play to fill the visual gap. Their bare delights are "purity and evocative." A spectacular, flaming image – since it threatens their critichood need to be able to write – is bad and they attack it throwing in moral extensions and hinting at idiocy in whoever is capable of visually appreciating a visual medium. Montez-land is truly torn down and contemporary sports-car Italians follow diagrams to fortunes, conquests, & murders to universal approbation.

Maria Montez was a particular person:
Off screen she was:
A large, large boned woman
5'9"
Oily
Skin dark
& gave impression of being
dirty
Wore Shalimar perfume

It is a reminder of one's own individuality to value a particular screen personality. It is also a nuttiness (because gratuitous). But you will have nuttiness without Maria Montez – want more – need all you can get – need what ever you don't have – & need it badly – Need what you don't need – need what you hate – need what you have stood against all through the years. Having a favorite star has very human ramifications – not star-like entirely. Stars are not stars, they are people, and what they believe is written on their foreheads (a property of the camera). Having a favorite star is considered ludicrous but it is nothing but non verbal communication the darling of the very person who doesn't believe anything real can exist between a star and a real person. Being a star was an important part of the Montez style. Having Maria Montez as a favorite star has not been gratuitous (tho it was in 1945) since it has left a residue of notions, interesting to me as a film-maker and general film aesthete. No affection can remain gratuitous. Stars who believe nothing are believable in a variety of roles, not to me tho, who has abandoned myself to personal tweakiness.

Those who still underrate Maria Montez, should see that the truth of Montez flix is only the truth of them as it exists for those who like them and the fact that others get anything out of them is only important because it is something they could miss and important because it is enjoyment missed. No one wants to miss an enjoyment and it is important to enjoy because it is important to think and enjoying is simply thinking – not hedonism, not voluptuousness – simply thought. I could go on to justify thought but I'm sure that wouldn't be necessary to readers of magazines. There is a world in Montez movies which reacting against turns to void. I can explain their interest for me but I can't turn them into good film technique. Good film technique is a classical attribute. *Zero de Conduite* – perfect film technique, form, length, etc., a classical work – Montez flix are none of these. They are romantic expressions. They came about because (as in the case of Von Sternberg) an inflexible person committed to an obsession was given his way thru some circumstance. Results of this sort of thing TRANSCEND FILM TECHNIQUE. Not barely – but resoundingly, meaningfully, with magnificence, with the vigor that one exposed human being always has – and with failure. We cause their downfall (after we have enjoyed them) because they embarrass us grown up as we are and post adolescent / post war / post graduate / post-toasties etc. The movies that were secret (I felt I had to sneak away to see M.M. flix) remain secret somehow and a nation forgets its pleasures, trash.

Somebody saved the Marx Bros. by finding
SERIOUS MARXIAN BROTHERS ATTRIBUTES.
Film for these film romanticists (Marx Bros., Von Stroheim, Montez, Judy Canova, Ron Rice, Von Sternberg, etc.) a place. Not the classically inclined conception a strip of stuff (Before a mirror is a place) is a place where it is possible to clown, to pose, to act out fantasies, to not be seen while one gives (movie sets are sheltered, exclusive places where

nobody who doesn't belong can go). Rather the lens range is the place and the film a mirror image that moves as long as the above benighted company's beliefs remained unchallenged, and as far as their own beliefs moved them.

If Maria Montez were still alive she would be defunct. She would be unable to find work (Maybe emasculated mother type parts) She'd be passé, dated, rejected. A highly charged idiosyncratic person (in films) is a rare phenomenon in time as well as quantity. Unfortunately their uniqueness puts a limitation upon itself. Uniqueness of Quantity calling into existence a uniqueness of time to limit itself. We punish such uniqueness, we turn against it – give it only about 5 years (the average life of a star). Once lost these creatures cannot be recovered tho their recovery would be agreeable. Who wouldn't welcome back Veronica Lake who is by this time a thing in the air, a joke, a tragedy, a suffering symbol of downfall, working as a barmaid at Martha Washington Hotels – shorn. We lose them – our creatures. When some rudeness / cutting off of hair out of fear of wartime machinery / makes the believer disbelieve, the believer joins us in our wanting but not being able to believe and is through, first because of the cynicism of movie fans and secondly because of the resultant breakdown of their fantasy.

Corniness is the other side of marvelousness. What person believing in a fantasy can bear to have its other side discovered. Thru accidents, rudenesses, scandals, human weaknesses have cut short those who made movie worlds (movies as place) that were too full to have room for anything but coincidences, politenesses & benightings. But denial is short lived. So will our denial of our personal films. Someday we will value these personal masterpieces. We don't have to do injustice to the film of cutting, camera movement, rhythm, classical feeling, structured, thought loaded (for there's the moldiness of the foreign darling, that it disobeys its own most central rule – that technique by itself can evoke as does poetry). Yet plots that demand serious definite attention spell out the evocation for the images.

On a very obvious level too much dialogue (still a violation even if it is no longer Hollywood-moronic) on an unsuspected level – much use of story furthering (different than Hollywood) images, rich with story furthering detail (more sophisticated than Hollywood details), rich with (more tour de force than H) cutting – all these exist not to create a film for itself but exactly the same effect as Hollywood Oprobriums – a film for a plot – all these tools of film STILL force an emphasis on the story because they each are used still to force an emphasis on the story and we only have a Hollywood disguised in sandals, Rivieras, palazzi, ascots, etc. A new set of cliches that we aren't familiar enough with yet to see as cliches. European films are not necessarily better than the most Hollywood of our flix, they are only different and that superficially – certainly not more filmic because they are every bit as / plot story work / oriented. This we will see clearly when we start to get tired of their particular set of thought & story cliches. And we must, because these are always oppressive in a film – are the oppressive parts of movies as we know them because they dissipate the film challenge – to use our eyes. To apprehend thru our eyes.

The whole gaudy array of secret-flix, any flic we enjoyed: Judy Canova flix (I don't even remember the names), *I walked with a Zombie, White Zombie, Hollywood Hotel*, all Montez flix, most Dorothy Lamour sarong flix, a gem called *Night Monster, Cat & the Canary, The Pirate,* Maureen O'Hara Spanish Galleon flix (all Spanish Galleon flix anyway), all Busby Berkeley flix, *Flower Thief*, all musicals that had production numbers, especially Rio de Janeiro prod. nos., all Marx Bros. flix. Each reader will add to the list.

Above kind of film is valid only when done by one who is its master – not valid in copies. Only valid when done with flair, corniness, and enjoyment. These masterpieces will be remembered because of their peculiar haunting quality – the copies will drop away from memory and the secret film will be faced. We still feel the disgust and insult of the copies and react against the whole body including the originals. The secret films were the most defenseless since they afford to ignore what bad copies caused us to come to its demand in order to protect ourselves from the bad copies. And they being the pure expressions have had to take all the blame.

A bad copy film has a way of evoking a feeling of waste that is distressing. Waste of time in months, money in millions – we spent our *own* best part of a dollar – and hope for more film excitement was made guilty in lying sequels – squandered money. The guilt has come to be applied to the flix that were copied. (Who will ever admit having enjoyed a Judy Canova flic?) The flix of the '30s and '40s (even I detest flix of the '50s) are especially guilty because they haven't acquired the respectability of antiquarianism. Anyway the secret flic is also a guilty flic.

These were light films – if we really believed that films are visual it would be possible to believe these rather pure cinema – weak technique, true, but rich imagery. They had a stilted, phony imagery that we choose to object to, but why react against that phoniness? That phoniness could be valued as rich in interest & revealing. Why do we object to not being convinced – why can't we enjoy phoniness? Why resent the patent "phoniness" of these films – because it holds a mirror to our own, possibly.

The primitive allure of movies is a thing of light and shadows. A bad film is one which doesn't flicker and shift and move through lights and shadows, contrasts, textures by way of light. If I have these I don't mind phoniness (or the sincerity of clever actors), simple minded plots (or novelistic "good" plots), nonsense or seriousness (I don't feel nonsense in movies as a threat to my mind since I don't go to movies for the ideas that arise from sensibleness of ideas). Images evoke feelings and ideas that are suggested by feeling. Nonsense on one given night might arouse contemptuous feeling and leave me with ideas of resolution which I might extend to personal problems and thus I might be left with great sense. It's a very personal process – thoughts via images and therefore very varied. More interesting to me than discovering what is a script writer's exact meaning. Images always give rise to a complex of feelings, thots, conjectures, speculations, etc. Why then place any value on good or bad scripts – since the best of scripts detracts most from the visual import. I suspect we are less comfortable in the visual realm than in the literary. Visual truths are blunt, whereas thots can be altered to suit & protect. The eye falls into disuse as a receiver of impressions & films (images) mean nothing without word meanings.

Our great interest in films is partly the challenge it presents us to step into the visual realm. A personality type star appeals to, informs the eye. Maria Montez was remarkable for the gracefulness of her gestures and movement. This gracefulness was a real process of moviemaking. Was a delight for the eye – was a genuine thing about that person – the acting was lousy but if something genuine got on film why carp about acting – which HAS to be phony anyway – I'd RATHER HAVE atrocious acting. Acting to Maria Montez was hoodwinking. Her real concerns (her conviction of beauty / her beauty) were the main concern – her acting had to be secondary. An applying of one's convictions to one's activity obtains a higher excellence in that activity than that attained by those in that activity who apply the rules established by previous successes by others.

The more rules broken the more enriched becomes the activity as it had to expand to include what a human view of the activity won't allow it to not include.

What is it we want from film?
A vital experience
an imagination
an emotional release
all these & what we want from life
Contact with something
we are not, know not
think not, feel not, understand not,
therefore: An expansion.

Because Maria Montez who embodies all the above cannot be denied – was not denied – the mass of thoughts we have about film must be added to, to include her acting, since anybody's acting is only the medium of soulful exchange and is not important in itself except at the point that the acting student learns to forget its rules; In Maria Montez's case a high fulfillment was reached without ever having known the rules and those who adore rules could only feel offense, and expressed it in ridicule.

M.M. dreamed she was effective, imagined she acted, cared for nothing but her fantasy (she attracted the fantasy movies to herself – that need-ed her – they would have been ridiculous with any other actress – any other human being). Those who credit dreams became her fans. Only actresses can have fans and by a dream coming true she became and actually was and is an actress.

(Go to the T.D. of the NYPL – go to the actress dept., ask for stills of "Maria Montez." Six Gigantic Volumes of delirious photos will come up on the dumb waiter.)

But in my movies I know that I prefer non actor stars to "convincing" actor-stars – only a personality that exposes itself – if through moldiness (human slips can convince me – in movies) and I was very convinced by Maria Montez in her particular case of her great beauty and integrity.

I finish this article – a friend, David Gurin, came to tell me "I came to tell you, tonight I saw a young man in the street with a plastic rose in his mouth declaiming – I am Maria Montez, I am M.M." A nutty manifestation, true – but in some way a true statement. Some way we must come to understand that person. Not worth understanding perhaps – but understanding is a process – not the subject it chooses. But that process has a Maria Montez dept. as well as a film dept. and you bought this magazine for a dollar.

Film Culture #27 (Winter 1962 – 1963)

1. The chief designer at Universal during the 1940's, Vera West was credited with creating the costumes for the most successful Maria Montez vehicles. West left the studio in 1947 (as did Montez) and was found, several months later, drowned in the swimming pool of her Hollywood home. A cryptic suicide note explained that she was "tired of being blackmailed." (J.H.)

THE MEMOIRS OF MARIA MONTEZ
or Wait For Me At The Bottom Of The Pool

The dust settled. O finally! Maria Montez was propped up beside the pool which reflected her ravishing beauty. A chunk fell off her face showing the grey under her rouge. How can we get to it? We must retrieve it or else scrape off all her flesh and start all over. Best to fish the chunk out of the pool and pat it back into shape. It'll show as a blotch on her cheek but we can shoot around that. Somebody will have to go out there with a pole.

The makeup lady is in back trying to bring Florence Bates back to life. She can't leave the butter churn or Florence may go rancid. Actually any clever character actress could play the makeup woman in chinese drag. We need all the character actresses to impersonate the staff which doesn't exist. They just went home. I hate to ask Charles to get up because he has a thousand strings going out of his asshole leading to everybody on the lot and would stir up so much dust and tear up his ass. O sit down, Charles . . . Come back, Oh he's stumbled against Miss Montez and his leg is snagged in her veils; the pole is lodged in her cunt. O she's all farted up now plus it'll be years before the dust settles.

We will go on with this scene; we'll pretend it's a sirocco scene and just restore Miss Montez's face. We'll have to use what's left of her leg because some of her face got stepped on. I'll put her in a voluminous cloak that will show only her face. The leading man can have his head buried in a chunk of her hair. That'll prop him up. Actually we could use some one alive in this scene because his face won't show but who could stand the smell from her decomposed body.

The love scene by the pool is finally being shot. There's no indication that the camera is working though. But if we had to worry about that we'd all go mad. We! I'm the only one here. The chunk of putrid meat in the pool showed up in all the shots.

The scaffolding around the vast Vapid Lot slipped. It rumbled and crumbled but didn't fall to the ground. More scaffoldings would be constructed around the crumbling scaffolding to keep it up. But the weight of the old scaffolding would weaken the new scaffolding and another crust of scaffolding would be built around the whole. Long ago the Movie Studio itself had fallen and now only repetition memories filmed themselves there. But the walls could never be located to be rebuilt if anyone cared to look as no one did because they had fallen into a powder among the maze of scaffolding. And the scaffolding was thick; it provided a thick wall of green darknesses behind which the entire lot strove incessantly to create a film the name and subject of which was forgotten long ago strove as in an endless hopeless dream to attempt to start to try to start this film with no personnel, a leading man dying of old age, a dead leading lady, a decomposing beloved old character actress, no leadership or funds, or coffee money but certain gorgeous color rouged subjective images and a couple of marvelous fantasticated, Etruscated, ruined sets.

The decor hangs down in tendrils and dust settles over all. There are strangled bodies hanging in the tendrils. They were the set decorators. They sway and moulder flaking, flaking. The tendrils disappear in a network of scaffolding.

The set disappears in shadows, disappears in scaffolding. Miss Montez has disappeared from view. She has sunk into the decor or it has sifted down on her. I think the scene should be shot anyway because she may be in there somewhere but we just can't see her but it'll come out on the film.

THE TAKE

A few layers of scaffolding are left standing. Maria Montez is chatting and smiling beside the white lily flowering pool. She is wrapped in white gauzy-mers. As she plays the scene the makeup lady furtively dabs makeup on her. She stumbles and leaves a red smear across Miss Montez's mouth, then the mouth falls off. The rouge pot falls on the set. Blend it out evenly! Don't stop the take. Miss Montez whips up a fan over her mouth for the rest of the take. She gets up and laughs in the leading man's face. He glows orange with makeup. The air around him is orange. His eyes, swimming with adoration, follow her. He touches her veil as she sweeps past him. Orange smear. His arm falls off. The fat makeup lady runs in and puts it back as a shower of white flowers swirls down to create a distraction Everything is going beautifully. Miss Montez poises for a moment on the stairs, one shapely leg coming out of her slit, pointing toward mecca on its gold kid ankle strap wedgie. She speaks her last line of dialogue her teeth glitter behind the fan. "Vait for me at the bottom of the pool." She runs down the stairs and a couple hundred white doves are released as she stumbles and rolls screaming down a million flights of stairs and the shot ends.

THE POOL

The leading man realizes he has been duped at the bottom of the pool. But the pool is beautiful. There are gorgeous aqua arabesques on the bottom and they wave in the water. In brilliant blue shadows actors drown. The scene steeps in gorgeous purples and above Maria Montez covered with rouge lowers her fan, grinning. Her eyes close and the makeup lady runs up and forces them open.

Rushes come back that no one remembers taking or how they fit into the movie. Rushes of blank film, of sets not on the lot, of empty, ruined, demolished sets. Sets with no people on them. The cameraman weeps. Endlessly long shots of deserted sets of preworld war Monte Carlo ballroom sets empty. Sets that never existed on the shambles lot.

Film Culture #31 (Winter 1963 – 1964)

BELATED APPRECIATION OF V.S.

People never know why they do what they do. But they have to have explanations for themselves and others.

So Von Sternberg's movies had to have plots even tho they already had them inherent in the images. What he did was make movies naturally – he lived in a visual world. The explanation plots he made up out of some logic having nothing to do with the visuals of his films. The explanations were his bragging, his genius pose, – the bad stories of his movies. Having nothing to do with what he did (& did well), the *visuals* of his films.

In this country the movie is known by its story. A movie is a story, is as good as its story. Good story - good movie. Unusual story - unusual movie, etc. Nobody questions this. It is accepted on all levels, even "the film is a visual medium" levels by its being held that the visuals are written first then breathed to life by a great cameraman, director. In this country the blind go to the movies. There is almost no film an experienced & perceptive blind man couldn't enjoy. This is true. I was a B'way barker once & was approached by a blind man! The B.M. was right – there must be others! The manager, nobody thought it strange – at the time I didn't – and don't now. I do think it strange that nobody uses their eyes. Occasionally a director will put in a "touch" – that can't be explained with words, needn't be, and this is always telling. But the literature of the film its words, trite, necessarily so far they are always doing something they shouldn't have to do, they are forced into triteness because they shouldn't be there at all – they should be in novels, anecdotes, conversations, etc. – (NO, movies are not conversations – why should they be so limited!) Music belongs, film is rhythm, so is music – if dialogue could be seen as rhythm it would belong. But just rhythm – not the printed page.

I don't think V.S. knew that words were in his way, but he felt it – neglected them, let them be corny & ridiculous, let them run to travesty

– and he invested his images with all the care he rightfully denied the words. And he achieved the richest, most alive, most right images of the world's cinema – in company with men like Von Stroheim, the genius of *Zero de Conduite*, early Lang & that limited company – Ron Rice today.[1]

His expression was of the erotic realm – the neurotic gothic deviated sex-colored world and it was a turning inside out of himself and magnificent. You had to use your eyes to know this tho because the sound track babbled inanities – it alleged Dietrich was an honest jewel thief, noble floozy, fallen woman etc. to cover up the visuals. In the visuals she was none of those. She was V.S. himself. A flaming neurotic – nothing more nothing less – no need to know she was rich, poor, innocent, guilty etc. Your eye if you could use it told you more interesting things (facts?) than those. Dietrich was his visual projection – a brilliant transvestite in a world of delirious unreal adventures. Thrilled by his/her own movement – by superb task in light, costumery, textures, movement, subject and camera, subject/camera/revealing faces – in fact all revelation but *visual* revelation. An example of how visual information informs. The script says Count so and so (in *Devil is a Woman*) is a weak character. The plot piles up situation after situation – but needlessly – Sternberg graphically illustrates this by using a tired actor giving a bad performance. If his hero is a phony for the purposes of the story, V.S. casts an actory actor in the part & leads him into hammy performance. Which comes to the acting in V.S. films. He got his effects directly through the eye. If the woman is deceptive he would *not* get Dietrich to give a great (in other words the convention of good acting wherein maximum craft conveys truthfulness) perf. of a woman conning. He would let her struggle hopelessly with bad lines she couldn't handle even if she were an actress. He let her acting become as bad as it could become for her. (A bad actor is rich, unique, idiosyncratic, revealing of himself not of the bad script. Select the right bad actor and you can have a visual revelation very appropriate to the complex of ideas and sets of qualities that make up your film. V.S. knew this and used bad acting regularly as a technique for visual revelation (not story telling).) For he was concerned with personal, intuitive, emotional values – values he found within himself – not in a script. With people as their unique selves, not chessmen in a script.

Possibly he might have been afraid of reaction if it were known that this visual fantasy world was really his own mind. He might have deliberately obscured, distracted attention from the shock that might have occurred if his creation had been understood through the eye. To close the ears would have thrown the viewer into an undersea, under-conscious, world where the realities were very different from what the script purported. He needn't have worried. As it was, no one had that ability to see. He was misunderstood and well understood. Well understood in that his covert world disturbed; Misunderstood in that no one knew why or appreciated the wonder of being disturbed. Misunderstood and done an injustice to in that finally when opinion turned against him it was for the wrong reason: (wrong not because people should not be disturbed) the insipid stories, bad acting, bad dialogue etc. Wrong reasons because they were, to be true to his expression, deliberately bad. Then he was punished – turned out of Hollywood and never again allowed to work. Only frightened people punish. Ostensibly because he had violated good technique. Good technique being used as something people hide behind when they are frightened by something they wouldn't like in themselves therefore is in themselves. And the hypocrisy of good acting, good this, good that – GOOD MOVIES being perpetuated – GOOD EMPTY – BANAL – UNTRUE MOVIES – IMPERSONAL MOVIES.

Film Culture #31 (Winter, 1963 – 1964)

1. Having made his underground reputation directing Taylor Mead's North Beach idyll in *The Flower Thief* (1960) and the beatnik road movie *Senseless* (1962), Rice featured Smith as an actor in *Chumlum* as well as *The Queen of Sheba Meets the Atom Man* – both in production around the time Smith wrote his tribute to Sternberg. By December 1964, Rice was dead – the 29-year-old filmmaker succumbed to pneumonia in Mexico. (J.H.)

JOURNAL NOTES ON *NORMAL LOVE*

Journal, 84:

July 23 – 1963.

O Cursed & Last & Evil days of summer of the bastard year 1963 – the FOGGY SUMMER OF WORSE troubles beset my path now than ever before when making FC. FC now history – undreamed of success met it – O because of that SAINT – Jonas Mekas.

The CURSED Yellow Sequence.

1. - Francine not home

2. - Got lost

3. - Francine not home

4. - Rained on JUST AS FRANCINE was putting finishing touches on her high drag.

O ITS THE LAST OF JULY! AND THE FOG ISNT LETTING UP AT ALL O MISS MONTEZ will this flic ever be finished? O HELP ME.

Journal, 89:

O Flic was actually completed to even my unbeleif (*sic*). I was a raving madman during last days of shooting. It shows on film which is totally insane – the actors all incandescently amok, no control over themselves – their souls glowing thru their skin. And their eyes burning with the desire to give & the realization of our common helplessness. Tragic twisted faces – Labrynths (sic) for a tormented Minotaur.

Journal, 110:

The pasty creatures leave the children's paradise and find regeneration in Bayberry Meadow and the mermaids heart is by the plump spider stolen away.

Journal, 65 – 67:

The HORRORS OF DEATH
Innocent Monsters
creatures come over hill
milk cows.

If Monday ever Comes, then I'll be Happy
Death in an Iron Door Clangs Shut
in form of a Broken Heart
The Dropping dead scene Shot
starts actors start their line &
slump thru shot to floor. Then
A montage of Dropping – extras
die towards end.
Normal Love.
Mummy tears curtain
Rene
piss
Diana disconsolate
mummy wanders
navel
intercut mummy plods – then jewel
Reclines on grass – then altar
Pasty at Reeds
Pasties face – green shot
shot of swamp
Diana comes in
Pasty runs across
pan shot
Dianas face
pan shot of LOTUS
Rene reclines & Pasty enters
RAPE
ALTAR
MUMMY PLODS
LAST OF FIREWORKS
for nights black nite scene – palanquin
arrives & woman places flowers on a grave
red & tail shot
mummy rips veil
fan lowers at mermaid

[a sketch of the spider appears here]
mummy rips off veil
FAN descends
Rene nave – dark
all those shots
veil off
deflowerment
scene in [*deleted*: pool] MUD
fireworks
pink werewolf
fireworks
descends on mermaid & fireworks
after mermaid is raped
MUMMY PLODS
Then wanders
Then 1st shot of cobra scene

Journal, 106-107:
cobra milking
arrival with melon
dance
milk bath – turning on
John Flies
John pouts
pink and green milk
John climbs in milk
John dances
The Moldy Hell of Men & Women
cobra milking
eat
arrives back with milk
dancing shot
watermelon arrives
eat watermelon
then drink pink & green milk

out of focus shot milk bath
then Francis picks over melon
Francine picks over melon
they dance
run off

Journal, 194 – 195:
April 1963 version CINEMAROC
Pasty Thighs
Sun (pink and green) comes up
creatures come trailing over the hillside
shot of the green pool pink flowers around it – at end of shot lite starts
to flicker faintly
They go into milk shed
They milk cows & cast raging glances back and forth, somebody gags on
milk as lite starts to flicker (she dashes her milk on him) – gr. mummy
tries to paw the snake woman – is repulsed
WL leaves cow shed
Slavey puts melon on ground by pavilion
WL runs through woods
Slavey runs through woods cut abruptly:
They are seen in still plastique by swing
The pool bubbles
The mongo watches the melon.

The green mummy watches the mongo
The light on the melon flickers in C.U.
The light on the mongo flickers in C.U.
The light on the melon flickers in C.U.
The light on the mongo flickers in C.U.
The swinging sequence
she swoops off swing and they roll in grass (black on white)
The snake lady dances then rushes off and is strangled by mummy . . .
B&W rolling
The mongo rushes to the melon and stuffs it up.

The preceding notes concern the making of *Normal Love*, or *The Great Pasty Triumph*, as it was briefly known. They include scenes that were realized, if at all, in somewhat altered versions. Among those named in the text: Rene is Rene Rivera, billed as Delores Flores in *Flaming Creatures*, and as Mario Montez thereafter. John Vaccaro, of the Playhouse of the Ridiculous, appears as The White Bat in later sequences, and is also credited in the titles as Pink Fairy, a role shared by Francis Francine. Pasty is Arnold Rockwood, who also appears in *Flaming Creatures*. Diana is Diana Bacchus, who is billed as the Girl in the film.

Smith sketches the Claes Oldenburg cake with stick figures representing the "Chorus Cuties" dancing on its tiers. It is labeled PINK for the dominant hue of the scene, indicates the location at BAYBERRY MEADOW, includes an earlier title for the work, *The Great Moldy Triumph*, and the judgment of its maker, SUCCESS. The drawing is placed in a spread that is otherwise dominated by sketches for the almond blossom tree set for *Flaming Creatures*. At Smith's request, Oldenburg had provided a model for the cake's fabrication. The model survives. (E.L.)

"Ray & Bonnie"

NORMAL LOVE

Early that morning I could see that the day would be an ordeal. The Cretins were most excitable and openly masturbated, overstimulating the pinheads. Today they would put on their shepard and shepardess costumes and run across the fields with their sand pails to milk the cows. I rode shotgun on them in my floor length black leather jacket and needle-heeled opera hip boots made of wildebeest leather with the tufted tops.

I lingered over my toilette, admiring my enormous three foot long 9 inch thick cock; I posed before my glass, throwing my cock first over this shoulder, then the other. Finally, overstimulated, I fucked my tufted tops on my boots. However, I was unsatified so I lunged at my mirror my noble horsecock all tumescent. I smashed through the mirror and whirled about and stuffed my cock into the jagged hole and fucked and fucked. My cock got all bloody and torn up. Then, to get maximum sensation out of it I stomped my cock in my boots, flinging handfuls of meat tenderizing salts upon it.

Herding the freaks across the fields, a fly alighted upon my cheek and I became concupiscent again. I prodded a pretty young marshmallow cretin girl with my crop and made her sprawl on the ground. Her hoop skirt flung up exposing her dimpled pasties. In a second I was upon her nudging her between the buns with my lobolier. She squealed and rolled upon her back thrusting her pouting quim into my face. I whipped out my flaming organ. Her hoopskirt was up over her face and she couldn't see. I ran back a few paces, aimed my cock-O and charged her but my horse galloped in before me and impaled her on his raging rod. Slightly disappointed I charged my horse's asshole and jumping up I transfixed him in mid-air as he was transfixing the cretin girl. My cock sank deliciously into his bowels, reaming them out straight and he reared and bolted causing me to spend even more deliciously. The little cretin shepardess was now ruined for normal love and she ran amok among the other freaks, inflaming them. Soon the whole hillside was one gigantic, seething, cretin, mongolian and pinhead orgy. Delighted, I ran to where my horse lay and snatched my elephant gun off the pack. I opened up on the churning carnival of freaky sex, firing point-blank into its midst. Presently, I sank delirious to the ground, gasping and creaming and blazing away at the freaks.

God's plump buns rested serenely on the ziricorn & rhinestone throne & he frowned at us through his long gold beard. We were in heaven. He ordered us all to line up, turn around, drop our pants, and bend over. We meekly obeyed. God then walked up and down paddling us with a ping-pong paddle. He concentrated chiefly upon the plump pasties, I noticed. He began to emit giggles and rushed from pasty to pasty paddling shit out of them. The freaks became overstimulated and soon we were in the middle of a gang fuck which spread over all the heavens. Saints and cupids dicked each other with their wands, angels threw their legs open and the skies dripped come.

The End

The Floating Bear #28 (Christmas 1963)

For the Diane di Prima/LeRoi Jones (Amiri Baraka) publication *The Floating Bear*. Smith crafted a brief erotic revery, "Normal Love." The source for the piece is a journal entry in a section devoted to the making of *Normal Love* (pgs. 169 – 173). In the published text, Smith deletes a few tentative, concluding lines and occasionally recasts a phrase, among them one that changes "normal sex" to "normal love," introducing the film title as it would appear in general usage. In the journal, "The Embalmed Horsecock" – Smith's original title for the piece – becomes "THE TITLE God's Body." (E.L.)

THE ASTROLOGY OF A MOVIE SCORPIO

Sunday, Nov. 17 – I woke up this morning with as much joy and relief as a little white scorpion would feel coming out of the bad part of its zodiacal sign – around the middle of scorpio. Certain stars had shifted and I knew the pressure was off. I looked around and for once there was no damage. The curtains of my bedroom looked incredibly luminous. My transparent curving tail coiled and uncoiled slowly, with pleasure on the warm sheets. We scorpios had been having bad times with one another, It suddenly seemed we were a nest of scorpios. We realized this with horror early in November – that we had all fallen in together – all of us scorpios – all of us sharp as razors. I smoked a joint and jerked off and started to think clearly: I have a message for artists all over the world. Very often great artists are not understood, even by young intellectuals in other countries. I do not understand or like the work of Fernand Leger. Do not criticize if you don't understand. Someday even I may come to like the work of Fernand Leger. I hope so.

My birthday was just over. I am 31. I felt chilled among my warm sheets. Waking up one morning a 31 year old man throws a scare into one. Life is passing – I am dying. O God, let me live. Which was probably the first religious expression of my whole life.

But it's true that it was a bad time in the stars. Viola Vayne, a Ron Rice starlet threatening to commit suicide on the stage of the Gramercy Arts Theatre during a film co-op screening. After Rice told me this and left I realized I had forgotten to ask at which one, as there were three screenings 7:30, 9:15 and 11:00.

To the general public:
All of the beautiful and poetic young film-makers of the new american cinema have been making dirty, nude movies lately because we are told not to – naughty aren't we. You think so, you think we are naughty to look at bodies, think about our orgasms, apply the processes of our intel-

lect and imaginations to determining what the body's needs are, to be led by our bodies. You are led by your bodies, *Village Voice* Readers, whether you know it or not – Most of the terrible tensions of your lives come from the discrepancies between what your bodies ask of you and your crabbed gratifications. (Alright then, *Look* readers.) All the flaming young directors shot nude stuff this last summer. Naomi Levine made a movie wherein little kids swatted each other with armfuls of huge white flowers. And some of the kids pants were fallen down – revealing them . . . NAKED! . . . BOO!! Barbara Rubin has made a ballet of sexual organs movie, which you will never see, whether you would like to or not. Because you have given control to censors you cannot see this film by Barbara Rubin, an eighteen year old girl whether you might or might not decide that you can take it.[1]

Fall has sped by – too quickly for the film creatures to capture its colors on film. We haven't been very mobile, though we are trying to become more so through banding together and sharing facilities and information. Now we'll spend a while editing our summer footage – keeping it close against ourselves to warm us through the winter. Then there will be next season's eruption of nudity in films with all its attendant controversy, and discussion . . . no doubt heated.

After the sickeningly pasty reception in New York City of FLAMING CREA-TURES I was not likely to make another movie that the people of my own city couldn't see (not much gratification in that) so I spent my summer out in the country shooting a lovely, pasty, pink and green color movie that is going to be the definitive pasty expression. All the characters wear pink evening gowns and smirk and stare into the camera.

There are only two little moments of nudity in my new movie (which I call NORMAL LOVE). I hope they don't make me take them out. Due to the demands of the script I had to have a nude bathing sequence (I wrote the script). I tried to keep the actress covered with lotus leaves but they parted for a couple of seconds and there is this marvelous glimpse of the actress' exquisite breasts.

The other moment of nudity occurred during the shooting of the Great Pasty Birthday Cake by Claes Oldenburg scene when the actor who played Uncle Pasty neglected to bring his costume, a lace curtain, to the cake set which was a long trek into the woods. There was no time to go back and get it and I had to shoot him sprawling naked and dying and hamming in the sinking sun, being sprayed with water by the Mongo gone berserk with his water machine gun as all the pasty cutie pie chorus creatures sprawled screaming on the layers of the 12 foot high cake. Among the cutie pies on the cake was Diane di Prima, the poetess, clad in a g-string and nipple coverers and nine months pregnant in a rough and dangerous scene. Four hours after we got back to N.Y.C. from location in Connecticut, Diane went into labor that produced a baby boy, Alexander Hieronymus Marlowe. I guess Diane just decided she wanted to be in that scene. She is a Leo.

Now to prove to you that I know what I am thinking about and that I have every right in the world to make a movie called NORMAL LOVE, I'll tell you something about normal love.

People should be able to caress each other during their quarrels. Then their quarrels can really be passionate. Scorpios: be jealous and quarrel on, that is your nature. We must be humorous, fair and affectionate even while we quarrel . . . the tender part of life depends on it. We can achieve this balance because we are incredible.

Posthumously published in *Film Culture* #76 (June 1992) which dates the piece 1964, although it was evidently written in November 1963.

Film Culture notes that it was prepared by Smith for the *Village Voice* at the invitation of Jonas Mekas, but rejected for publication by staff editors. Both diaristic and epistolary, the text is cobbled together out of a number of entries in a loosely structured journal kept by Smith in the early 1960s. The section here addressed "To the general public" appears in the generally undated diary and in the form of a letter from Smith to Mekas's "Notes On Some New Movies and Happiness," *Film Culture* 37 (Summer 1965), reprinted in *Film Culture Reader*. Omitted in the published version is Smith's interjection: "Normal Love I thought. Very often great." The journal itself is part of the Jack Smith Archive. (E.L.)

1. Smith is referring to *Christmas on Earth* (a/k/a *Cocks and Cunts*) made by then-teenaged Barbara Rubin, Jonas Mekas's militant cohort in the promotion of *Flaming Creatures*. Far and away the most sexually explicit underground movie to date, Rubin's single opus would be known throughout the '60s largely by reputation. (J.H.)

"I KNEW HE WOULD NEVER COME TO ME . . ."

Journal, 191 – 190 (c. 1963)

I knew he would never come to me, though his heart was breaking and he knew mine most certainly was. So I stayed in my chambers and alternately wept, and raged, and talked to myself, to god and to him, but I made no move toward him because I knew he would make none toward me. Thus I punished him and myself for loving as adamant and unworthy a person as he. I toughened and strengthened myself for I would need to draw upon new made strength to see me through remorse and wretchedness my weakness had gotten me into. Thus I had rapidly to make strength to rapidly find it. I was able to do it because I had a perfect exemplar, my lover, my counterpart – my mirror image in suffering and strength, as a magician possessed of devils as I saw myself to be to feel these cruel fictions.

After every outrageous attack I would wonder – Does he still love me? Is this the end of his love? Now will it end? How many times will this occur before I lose his love? "O Doctor," I cried, "I know this is moldy thinking." "There, there," my psychiatrist cooed attempting to calm me. "Proust's sentences were as studied as they were out of his horror of syntax error. His fear that he might commit an error in grammar. Did anyone ever find a grammatical error in a Proust sentence?" he said, to divert me.

"Doctor," I said, "I repulsed my lover finally & forever with an inhumanly cruel note." "Do you want to tell me what it was?"

"Born of a hostile cunt, you are a perambulatory armory yet you do not fight but only take unfair advantage. Your pockets bristle with knives for every purpose. You do not express any regret because you feel none when a member of your household cuts himself on your preternaturally sharp table knives! You seethe with hostility in your lover's arms. I was your lover."

O! Orange clamato fuzz
Regardez
mon
clitoris, Clown
Clown come
of Capitalism

RED ORCHIDS

PFEFFERNUS FLAVORED ASPIRIN

Pfeffernus flavored aspirin was found to be hideously dangerous. Babies the size of strawberries were being born to women who were known poppers. These babies had enormous heads the size of spoiling watermelons and whispered obscene remarks in sibilant Levantine waterfront pidgin. They had lidless eyes and leering flaccid mouths. They were born in pierced ears. Some were even born with garish metallic paper carnival hats. Their mothers felt repugnance at the lewd comments they uttered at breast feeding time. Their limbs were unsightly thin and curling tendrils like withered asparagus bottoms which were covered with a fine prickly hair like on okra; and coiled and uncoiled continuously. When these tendrils were pinched off they grew right back clutching insulting greeting cards.

U.S. government mercy stations were set up to give the mothers free classes in stringing donut necklaces and pasting sequins on prune pit jewelry. The creatures required maple syrup and clorox enemas every half hour. Some mothers got prune pits stuck in the enema tubing and their babies died amid horrid screams and rectal explosions of white hot enema mixture. Many mothers dressed their babies elaborately in lace and spangles to over-compensate for the deformities. Some of the little creatures had 10 story high feathered headdresses. Sometimes these headdresses got snarled in high voltage telephone wires and the mothers would look down into the toddlers to see their babies incinerated like so many blackened and dehydrated ostrich droppings. Often nice old ladies would peer into the baby carriages to tweak their cheeks and would instead vomit into the carriage adding another knife into a mother's heart as she pushed the brimming carriage all the way across town in a raging hail storm. How could a mother hold down her job as a nightclub chanteuse and take care of the baby too? In desperation she took it around to commercial photographers to pose for telephoto close-ups of flaccid anal openings.

One Norwegian avant-garde literary review bought one of the pictures for an account of the *Andrea Doria* sea collision. The *Stockholm* rammed her amidship. The *Andrea Doria* listed 45 degrees because she was top heavy due to the fact that the hold had been emptied of its cargo of Shalimar perfume. The first class passengers had been permitted to swim in it but it was discovered that a senile silent movie aquatic queen had not been coming out of the Shalimar when she had to pee. The liner was therefore made topheavy. She was due to come into New York the next afternoon. She was skimming through the night at a snappy clip. The last drop of Shalimar trembled on the lip of her bilge pumps and shook off into the foaming Atlantic. Then there was a hideous crunching and splintering sound and a shudder racked the unlucky boat. The pointed prow of the *Stockholm* had dildoed a gaping hole in her side. A startling and different freak effect had occurred. A fat middle aged lady had been sleeping bare ass in the top of a double decker bunk and the unusually spoon shaped prow of the *Stockholm* had acted as a pancake flipper and had scooped her up and flipped her onto the wreckage that had been its own prow.

The poor woman sat facing in toward the ship perched near the edge among the tangled entaglio. Her red hair fell down over her shoulders, her beer belly bobbled from side to side. In the gray disastrous light she seemed luminous and vaguely nacreous. One of the crew risked his own safety to crawl out to haul her in. Not till he almost reached her did he realize that she was dead. He noticed a ring with a large blue stone upon one hand. He reached out for her hand to haul her in but her entire arm came off when he jerked on it. He released the arm and it dropped into the water. He fought down the horrors and reached out for her hair to drag her in by that means. Agony and nausea fought for supremacy in his brain which was about to burst into flames. The woman's hennaed tresses came out in his grasp. There was no way he could pull her off now so he crawled back racked with agonized revulsions and stunned by this encounter with the overt hideousness of life on earth in all of its beastliness. Later that chunk of prow fell off dragging the mysterious woman with it. She was instantly devoured by a great many sharks which had been waiting about below. The water was lashed into a froth of frenzied foam.

The monstrous baby investigations threw up startling revelations. Many housewives were raging dope fiends; they were continually up on reducing drugs which were shockingly high in amphetamines and spirit lifters. They would get together in the daytime and get high as kites and laugh. Many college girls either imagined they did or actually got high on Dristan. The debased pseudo-artistic scum that infest decomposing N.Y. tenements made tea of asthma cigarettes and experimented with mold florets found on putrescent pussy sweetener. Debbie Reynolds claimed that the mystery woman was her scrub-woman who had been junketing about in Europe. A special line of cosmetics then appeared on the American market for the monstrous spawn. They sat up in their 18th century swan beds and applied enormous globs of the new chunky style non-gummo phantom of the opera face disfiguring pock hole filling smegma extracted from oversexed suitcase handles with new non-baby chaffing Posner's gazelle spunk with shredded movie magazines and broken glass, all foaming and hissing, scraped out of the tiny sperm thirsty cracks in sliding boards down which plummeted HOT and SCREAMING LITTLE GIRLS!

PASTY THIGHS

There was this old man who was the 2nd millionth assistant electricity grip and for 80 years he had clung to the top girder that over-hung the set. His job had been to shoot a little beam of light down onto the leading cunt's thigh providing the highlight thereof. It was ironic as hell. She got younger and younger every year and he got older and nastier. When he used to be able to see her thighs he would get erections but because he was straddled up on the girder the erections would be mashed backwards into his stomach causing deep wounds and causing him to fall screaming and coming off the girder onto the set. The leading cunt, Mavis Davis, would stare down at his mangled body and let off supercilious laughs and get 10 years younger.

After he had fallen off a few times he couldn't even see down to her thighs anymore and the highlight used to wander but nobody noticed or cared as his whole existence didn't matter shit to anybody anyway. But the old fuck would get hot anyway because the flapping sounds underneath him from all the grips watching her and jerking off made him hot anyway. He was being turned into a dirty homo by the most sexy goddess of all time. They were shooting on Pouting Quim when the old fart had his next to last hard on. The steel girder made it ram him through the stomach and displace his spine and he shot off into his head and he fell screaming off the girder with red hot come streaming out of his eyes and nose and mouth and ears and he fell thousands of feet trailing ribbons of come past layers of girders and creaming grips.

This time there was practically nothing left to hoist up to the thigh highlight spot but a basket of different body parts a few fingernail clippings, a pocket comb, etc. and just this little finger snaggled up out of the basket and controlled the spotlight. But now that his brain had snapped the old fart played madly tweaky tricks with his spot light. The thigh light wandered inanely all over the set producing mad thigh impressions all over everything, causing movie patrons to look at chairs, and chunks of the set and think of thighs. Then the thigh light came to rest because of some insanely perverse tweakiness upon Mavis Davis' tit. It made it look lopsided and she had to go under surgery on the foam rubber causing production to be held up for hours and costing untold millions and when they got her back on the chaise lounge her head looked too big. Foam rubber lobotomies, and so forth causing Mavis to get more lovely and youthful every minute and foam rubber and perfect and gorgeous and blonde and the Old Fart's finger got more and more bitter, and wrinkled and splenetic.

Finally Mavis died of old age as she got so young in the movie that they were shooting her birth. They pulled her out of this teenage character actress' womb in her clean evening gown a corpse. They had a huge funeral which was purported to be an advance press shower. There were more makeup men than people at the funeral and the eyelash tweaking section alone outnumbered the mourners much less the population of L.A. She was universally acclaimed the loveliest corpse in the form of an unborn female ovary to somehow not have been born yet but to have been the oldest illegitimate great grandmother of abortions over a period of 90 years. Her abortions alone because of the laws of averages 70 of whom grew up to become old hag character actresses never having existed because she got so young she disappeared backward sucking movies back 80 years before Georges Méliés with her, causing the non-existence of two generations of the world's population. Thus while the whole world didn't exist so the old Fart, manipulated by pulleys and cables strung all over the scaffolding on the set came down and nobody saw him much less existed while he snatched Mavis out of her coffin and laid a huge turd in it. This turd he had saved up for 150 years because his digestive along with his respiratory system had been shot so long. Her supercilious laughs he thot.

All manipulated by millions of pulleys all over the studio, hooked up to the studio dynamos and extension cord dept. his finger dragged her to the Siren of the Cretan Cookoo Cult set. Which had Cretan Egyptian pillars holding up birthday cake layers and Greek temples and there were no top layers because the top of the set was a little painting on a piece of toilet paper hanging close to the camera. In the middle of the set was the High Louis 16th Victorian altar – a triple life size cookoo clock. The old fart ironically laid her there because that was her next flick as the cookoo came out and cookooed inanely. The old fart violated her all over gushing come into her peplum, her chignon up the open toes of her ankle strap platform wedgies and cunt. Thus came to a flaming climax the raging bitter spiteful decade-spanning hate drenched bitter dramatic and dangerous love hate come smeared relationship mostly dramatic that ended so bizarrely as the cookoo trumpeted its weird cat calls. All the people on the set came up and ran up the stairs of the screaming wild assorted enraged mob cries and torches. So the old fart snatched out the lights. He ran out into the street carrying a sequined sanitary napkin, all that was left of Mavis. His finger was all exhausted by all that come gushing out from under its finger nail and was reduced to a hangnail which violated the holes of the sequins all supported by a thousand tons of cables and wires pouring out of the entrance of Moldie Studios which was struck down by a garbage truck putting an end to the flaming saturnalia of pinhead sex. The extras all ran up and stared down in horror at the pap smear right there in the middle of the street. They flung torches on it to stop the supercilious ecstasy moans.

The garbage truck swayed entangled in the cables and glittered thigh lights all over the blonde maggots that swarmed out of the turd in the coffin and crawled twinkling in their tiny silver lamé evening gowns all over the leading man, drinking leading man spot light sweat from his pores and basking in gigantic shimmering floods of toe to hands up thigh and cunt Sunday Coney Island Sunlight Daylight.

THE GREAT MOLDY TRIUMPH

The roly poly flotilla girls manned the bridge of the gleaming new luxury liner, the S.S. *Francis Francine*. The *Francine* had been famous in wartime for masquerading as a floating lady finger and, when surrounded by enemy ships, erupting into a smokescreen bubbles as her spunky aqua-marines pulled out their plugs. After the war she was converted into a luxury liner and massaged over the scalp with a champagne bottle and all hung with costume jewelry she slipped into the bubbly briney and the tap dancing flotilla girls saluted smartly, their hairy scrotums mashed up under their spangled dance panties.

The ship floated on the lapping Atlantic tweaked by the moon between nascent continents. Tides that wash and lap like old bubble backwash, if the world could be considered the inside of a washing machine – with no clothes, no soap, no paddles.

This mood of frivolity, that the world and everything in it is a mess of moldy laundry alluring grinding away like a rusty 1910 washing machine – its churning interior hypnotizing children that stare into them like a bird flying through corridors of space ape mop water (man is not yet Man) pulled by the tide through the foaming slosh, pin pointed back as the whole cold ocean pulsated small again then breaks and crashes against the porthole of the washer with furry noses pressed against it and the clotted, seething lace panties and scanties all silk and pink and brown stained, fermenting and storming, and heaving and exploding in giant waves that threaten to extinguish libraries the S.S. *Francine* floated giddy like some gilded bedroom slipper in an ocean of weltschmerz. O, what can save the tweaky sequined slipper from sadness!

Streamers draped about phonographs morning glories that thrummed in all the cabins – all playing Jane Powell's record of the oceana roll – a bubbly girl who I wish would be in more musicals . . . I'm the only one who is faithful to my movie stars . . . Old movies were shown in the theatre of the *F.F.* in the evening. Maria Montez flicks were the most shown, also Judy Canova flicks were popular. Usually there was no one on the bridge at such times or even ever and the flotilla girls were usually down in the bilge with the stokers and that breed of creatures who with posited the true truth that the unribald should be told at an early age that wisdom that mothers are sure preachers don't know about – causing them to smile in church and indeed go to church and some women's pussys can only go untense on a church pew. If a preacher some Sunday should say, "A stiff dick has no conscience," so many pussys would clamp up you'd think you were in a reverse explosion in a suction pump factory along the pews. Little boys would be taken home and their ears washed out with a blow torch.

But that never will happen. And the same mysterious thoughts that animate the preacher's clear forehead and make his brain a maze of neoprene tubing animate the phantom ropes that the basket cases swing on in the recreation room of the *Francine*.

Night – Francis Francine, the great lady who I herein suggest be made a saint because of her martyrdom, gilded on vaselined feet – quietly – through the darkened basket case starry sky watching ward and administered cold cream hand jobs. But quietly O so quietly so as not to galvanize them into shock. Some the great heart plugged in – the ones that had that much left on them and let them spend to death in a mercy creaming. However she went, baskets brimmed over and swung heavy on their ropes. For those who had nothing to play with she hit over the head with a cucumber. To those who dared to dream impossible dreams she showed them the sexes of 2 bodies on one and told them some fabulous carny gilded memories full of charming arabesques of speech and wise homilies and dignity and beauty. Plus she'd do the kooch she did on the bally only much more uninhibited, and there in the dark basket ward, almost in secret, as a little eruption between friends not because there were any movie cameras around, the apex of human bubbliness would foam up. Then she would put a little dab of cold cream on the nose tippo of the basket case and leave it enchanted. Even in those with pudendums this blossoming of etiolated snow crystal and mold floret bouquets transcended spermy thoughts, and left all charmed and with limp dicks.

Which was too bad when it was unintentional. But usually the bubbles would foam up through the jammed up sperm with corn starch in it and bubbles would riddle the gloppy spunk pudding.

Angel of Mercy or flirt? All was quiet now on the boat except uproarious screams from every dark corner and bawdy outcries, and ecstasy moans. The moon bloomed suffusely into the basket room. There was nobody on the bridge. The ship listed quite a few degrees. All of Francine's mother's furniture and belongings were on the boat, doilies, costume jewelry, vases, dresses, etc. and boxes and boxes of other things that could be given away all jammed the lifeboats and corridors and ballroom of the boat. That was Francine's martyrdom – she martyred herself for her mother to keep up her memory, her mother's kitchenette set, became her mother. The basket cases were men she had had a crush on at one time, yesterday's ecstasy.

We are all of us a bubble that makes transatlantic random voyages. Nature endows bubbles as well as mother of pearl with pink and green sparkling lights. There are those who see the bubble and the pink and green sparkles remain on their eyes. These are they who see brooches in snowflakes, mistake a glob of snot on the sidewalk for a rhinestone, find earrings while taking the air, and catalogue the tiny pin points of light. Any reflection bigger than 2 inches is not a highlight and is in the domain of others and noticed, recorded, analogized by them. All of us have lives, waste time, procreate, and more or less die depending on our health more than what we think about. Sadly, bubbles burst. But the Socratic part of bubbles stay on and a ravaged bubble is a magnificent thing. The pink and green go . . . but reappear all over the place, in startling ways. A milky interior of a milk bottle looks blue and orange if held to a light bulb. The yellow decade was also called the mauve decade. There is a mad woman of royal blood who wears a grinning death skull brooch of diamonds and she talks to it and they have elaborate conversations. No one can decide which is more beautiful of them or if they are beautiful. The brooch pulsates between hideousness and ravishing beauty. The mad woman, Baroness Horsecock, eats nothing but breast milk of butterflies and has the most rarified taste of her time. She is not an ape. She served free chicken and soup in her kitchen and has instituted in her domain the practice of thriftshop exchange, and bed unit social structure. She is quite old and is cheerful and keeps her pussy clean. She owns a boat which she sails about the Atlantic for her pleasure. The name of the boat is the S.S. *Antoine Pevsner* after the splendid sculptor. Countess Horsecock is convinced that she will die.

But does anyone really believe such a thing? The Baroness spent a lot of time at her only eccentricity, a crystal ball. She would put her death head brooch under it and it would loom up magnified and scary and she'd shift her head slightly from side to side and make the forms of the skull shift. She was a brave woman and she fascinated herself rather than scared herself by such tomfoolery. Ultimately she saw that she was pretty funny and she would let off loud bursts of laughter that could be heard all over the boat and even out at sea. These laughs chilled and petrified the crew with horror and all the sea gulls within earshot were immobilized with terror and dropped straight out of the air into the sea to drown.

One night the Baroness looked into her crystal ball and saw Francis Francine's face. Francine was lancing a pimple. Actually she may have been piercing her ears but a penis is rather blunt even if it is tumescent and she could get spattered with come. The Baroness started to play with her pussy and in her clumsiness, ruptured her cherry. It had been growing tough and thick and was more like a leather satchel than a cherry. She was secretly delighted; now she could really ovulate, and go swimming, and get over her foolish phobia of picket fences, popsickle sticks, and cucumbers. She wanted to show her pussy to everybody. When she entered the mess that night every one at once noticed her sparkling eyes, flushed cheeks, her yellow hair and pretty party frock, the skirt of which she held over her head. An old gentleman from whom she was hoping to receive funds for her projects had been secretly fucking the mashed potatoes during grace and shot his load and slumped under the table. A 5 lb. chunk of atrophied maraschino cherries shimmered as it slid down her leg and slid across the floor and overboard where it bobbled about in the water.

The startling red phosphorescence was spotted by a roly poly morphadike in the crows nest of the *Francis Francine* and reported to Francine. She was lowered on a rope to the water and cried out, "O cherries, but how different. They're not really in season!" She impaled a chutz of cherries on a miniature fork and popped it in her mouth. "OOO," she squealed, "Who done it and run!" She made her eyes go cross-eyed and patted her chest daintily. She was hauled up to the deck and seemed more or less normal except that she seemed to have bushier pubic hair and her beard was heavier and unwanted face hair was growing up around the sequins on her evening gown. She went to her private rooms and stared into her mirror, but unwanted pubic hair grew up around the mirror. Like the phoenix from the cocoon she emerged from the cabin. All were startled by her new efflorescence. She was little, had thin legs, small hard breasts and her fangs were yellow and hollow. She made flash predatory raids upon the roly poly girls.

She mistook their thighs for food. Mmm, chicken soup, she said as she chewed off one of their legs. Mmm, carrots, she said as she tore a chunk out of a red haired beauty's neck. Mmm, etc.etc. She painted over the name *Francis Francine* and retitled the ship the S.S. *Gilded*, raging screaming horror. She ran up to the crows nest and gobbled him up. Now for a refraisement she tore the cigarette machine apart and gobbled up its contents.

Termites? said the Pirate queen, Maria Montez as she sighted the floating shambles in the telescope of her galleon. "OOO," said Miss Montez, "I've never been in a pirate movie, unless you include *The Pirates of Monterey* which was basically just a 2 bit western that Universal threw up to capitalize on my name." Miss Montez steered her galleon oared by a hundred sweating Yvonne De Carlos straight into the S.S. *Gilded Screaming* etc. Miss Montez swung aboard and held off the were-Francine at sabre point. "Geef me your treasure" she cried. Francine lay down on the deck and spread her legs open, leering coyly.

"O," cried out Baroness Horsecock. She was looking in her crystal. "I shall have to save Francine. CHIVALRY, you know!" The Baroness steered her boat to the Francine's rescue. Maria Montez saw the Baroness' boat bearing down upon her and leaped back into her own. Uttering a thousand curses she steamed off toward Africa.

The two, Francine and the Baroness faced each other at last. "Alas poor creature," cried the Baroness and watered Francine with her tears.

Then O wonder of wonders, Francine became a man, Frankie, and the two flew into each others arms as halved souls unite after witches dissevered them at birth.

Frankie eventually absorbed the baroness and attained Sainthood, Manhood and Death all in the same instant!

Film Culture #33 (Summer, 1964)

OR "WHITE AGENT"

The White:

Pig of

Medina

A Light Bath

with Music

THE WHITE PIG OF THE MEDINA

The big greasy silver lead scorpion lived in the same room with the white pig of the medina. It laid there like 300 pounds of rancid lard & looked at her with its tiny ruby eyes. The room was chalky white except her part of it which had turned yellow. What had turned the white pig's part of the room yellow was leprosy and syphilis. The yellowness hung over her in these last and evil days. It turned her makeup yellow. She fondled her moldy, leprosy infected 8 x 10 glossies of herself taken when she was mounting toward stardom.

The white pig spent a lot of time compulsively scrubbing the room, as do many whores who have syphilis. She had to keep scrubbing. Maybe she endlessly smeared the diseased mop water around for nothing. Had the scorpion been shitting in the mop water? Blue-green shit bars certainly bobbed about in the mop water. "As long as a woman has that thing between her legs she can always make it," she thought but even Arab men didn't want to stick their zubs in there anymore.

"I'm a woman with morals," she would squall while being flipped over on her stomach and her flaccid, grayish white anus collapsed with a crash to the scrawny Arab man's enormous black horsecock of pleasure. He was a purveyor of powdered grasshopper aphrodisiac which he sold to the boys who live as women. He hung about in their quarter and did errands for them also. He boasted to them that he was laying a white actress as they put the ground grasshopper on their eyelids.

Pouting, pouting, pouting the Tangier afternoon slipped by like blue-veined things seen from the window of the white pig's room, seen through the yellowed afternoon air in the white pig's stucco plaster room. The crafty scorpion muffled a few semi-liquescent farts out of consideration for the white pig so as not to throw her into the horrors. We have to live with each other.

A dilapidated cardboard box with three stale cream-puffs was found, after a year, outside her door on the floor. They were filled with ostrich smegma, a powerful aphrodisiac and antiseptic. The white pig gobbled them all up.

The greedy whore now rolled panting and moaning on her bed heedlessly crushing the 8 by 10's. She stumbled to the window and hung her legs out in order to attract men in the street. But when they saw those big bubbles of puss oozing out of her pussy they knew the end was near. The scorpion shifted uncomfortably. He was afraid she'd fall off of the window; all he could see was her orange fingernails.

She had slipped too far out, that much was certain. Besides, the window ledge was slippery with pussy sweetener. She had hung a leg or two out of the window to attract men before, but this was too unbelievable. Nevertheless, the Scorpion took the opportunity to slip over to the mop pail and hastily and messily crawled defecating over it. Presently the Arab came in and looking around, was startled to find her not in. He sat on her bed to wait. There was fresh sweat on what was once a sheet. He sniffed the air – he knew that there was pussy nearby – the Scorpion felt a cold chill for the first time in its life . . .

The Arab's lever of Bagdad throbbed like an inflated inner-tube into erection and drained the blood from the rest of his body, causing him to feel faint and giddy. A tragic love story thus droned voluptuously on within the hotel room and just outside the window. One last climax.. . . the climax destiny meant them to have was being squandered stupidly. The White Pig hung rotting like some overripe moons of lard spoiling over the Medina while Arab ne'er do wells whistled and cheered and beat their meat in the street below. The Arab rolled the Scorpion over on its back, prodding for a body aperture. The Arab was lubricating in spurts now . . . the least contact with anything might unleash the spunky crescendo.

Many afternoons the hotel room had seemed to be under lemonade in the hot afternoon syphilitic light. The Scorpion had loomed pallid and pasty and yet dignified in its corner of the room slowly manufacturing the thin oil that exuded from its pock-marks. Its body temperature was always about 40 degrees. It got bigger year by year and had that pasty apathy immobility imparts. It had materialized out of the plumbing to nurture in the atmosphere of keif dreams that the White Pig gave up chunks of her putrefying body to maintain, swollen like the parasitic ends of a balloon that clamped on to the White Pig's tortured pleasure mounds. There are always vultures too fat and heavy to fly that brazenly squat around a slowly putrefying dream pretending to be somewhere else. No matter how long it takes to die these sloppy hairless buzzards can wait, having no projects of their own to dream about. And their eyes, like so many phony red emeralds, stare out and make one wonder if they really exist – so motionless are they. And all the while they are treacherously poisoning our very mop water.

The White Pig's knuckles were turned pink from the incredible strain of hanging there with all that lead weight hanging from them. Her eyes rolled up in her head, a shudder racked her quivering quim and her bowels emptied on the heads of the crowd of louts below that had been jeering at her passion. Her body stiffened, her legs flew apart, and her fingers relaxed their grip on the windowsill; her quim pouted wide open and caught a fly as she plunged to her death, screaming and streaming ribbons of spunk, the fly buzzing hysterically. The Buzzard's scorpion mask was bored into its skull as the Arab fucked it to death between the eyes and reamed it through and through 'til his drill blazed out of the Vulture's ass in a shower of Vulture shit at the end of the rainbow.

The Great Society (1967)

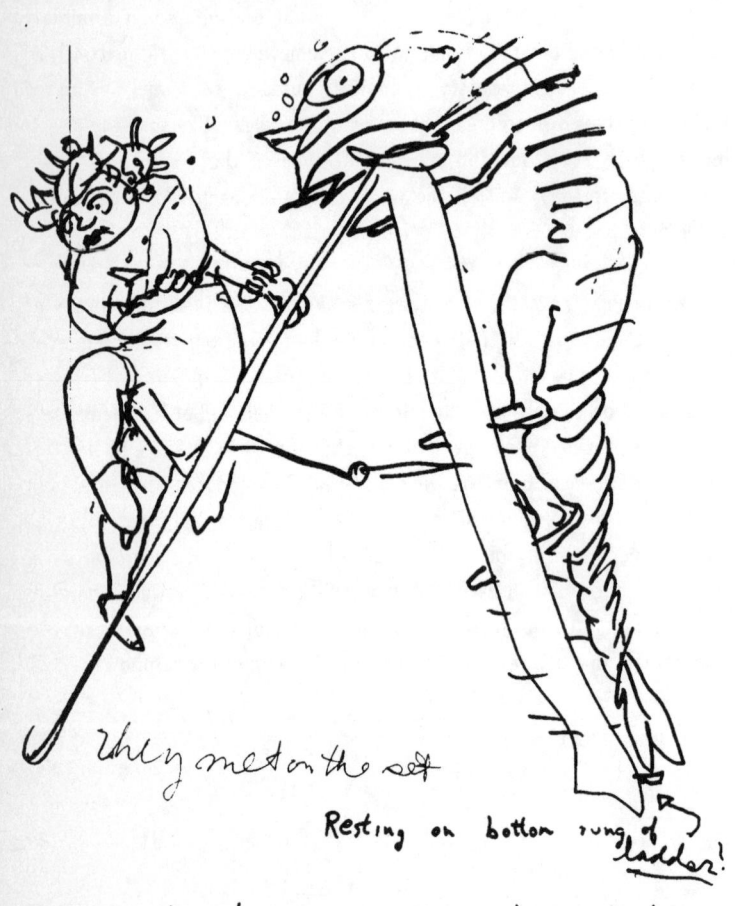

They met on the set

Resting on bottom rung of ladder!

Ther had met on the stepplader

JOURNAL NOTES ON THE USES OF PORNOGRAPHY

The adorable and pasty creatures find mass redemption and leave child-hood's Paradise. They leave their cake whereon they wasted their after-noons in the service of the forces of banality – the horror beneath the dreary, pasty face of every-day life of police protection and the sex fan-tasies of the manufacturers. But don't think they are obscene. All sex fantasies are equally valid. They are the means whereby the imagination leads the confused creature into sexual contact with other creatures which contact is difficult at best and can be impossible for the sensitive, the neurotic, the badly misinformed, the inexperienced, the young adults with very little in their experience that could provide a basis of rationali-ty. Sexual fantasizing is the pitiful means whereby the truly unpleasant difficult sex function is swathed in glamour, perversity, and ultimately, simply, interest. It is necessary for the propagation of the species and ergo soundness of consumer economy. That is why it seems strange that municipal-manufacturing interests give it the bad name of obscenity. Perhaps fetishists don't furnish homes, but in being driven into social guilt the dog who is most in the unrewarding thrawl adds to his thank-less and dry struggle to support a crushing imaginative structure the assuming of a bad name, even the unfair premise of being a dog. The real dogs are cynical, ugly men who pay off the municipal cynical, ugly men for the special right to present sun-bath movies, gross movies, meat magazines, strip-teasing, times square pulp fiction, 8 mm movies sold under counters along with plastic viewers and there are records too and vacant eyes but ugly because the police, the money collectors of the municipality are paid off, the ultimate acknowledgment by the involved parties of guilt – Devié bars, turkish baths, brothels and other institu-tions partake of this auto-acknowledgment and if there is such a thing as obscenity it is just this – the payment of funds to the police. The ugli-ness of this sly betrayal of self pervades necessarily the lives of the detectives, the businessmen, the officials, as it colors the lives of the consumers of this commodity. But pornography it is not – it is only a matter of levels of intelligence, sensitivity and maturity. The lowest possible levels of which the men who are our civil authorities place themselves upon by their choice of what they find attractive and repellent, vital, what they feel strongly enough about to tell the vital ambivalence inherent in payments which at once protect and punish. This protection-punishment is a feature of psychotic attachments and immature romances and the mortally distracted states of the unfortunates who are not immune wander dazed thru the steaming sexual delicatessen counter projection which is not really human but which is multiplied a millionfold almost into truth and which is apparently the ideal of beauty of our masters the manufacturers and which is swallowed whole by their lackeys the censors, the licensers, the police, and increasingly by a public which accepts the pasty foam rubber measurement darlings of panty ads as the consorts and determining image of their sex fantasy lives. Thus a concupiscent languor might logically be haunted by a can of pork and beans. Even this is not obscenity. Sex fantasy is deeply personal, nobody else's business, particularly not the business of Plutocrats whose proper sphere is finding new uses for plastic and the utilization of nubile girls for the necessary sexual act needed to tease extra pennies from a public which is happily milked for the sake of a steady flow of acquiescently grinning air-brushed darlings. The persual of the ads of any magazine turns into a sex fantasizing as it is intended by a vast mechanization. Persons have been known to lose sight of a personal imaginative, fanciful sex fantasy life of their own in this art department perfected dream-world of becoming gestures, poutings, affected rapture, and the dry, burning masks of raging psychosexual nymphomania that is accepted as a matter of course as the imaginations perfect love dumplings. And the nice manufacturers supply them in mind numbing quantities that makes philanderers of us all and causes some persons even to be shocked that there can exist sex fantasies other than seaminess of images of sexpartners not attired in brand new garments moments fresh from the dry cleaners, shocked by images of partners without textureless faces, shocked by the uselessness of anything but cut out, rigidly self conscious beings smiling pleasantly, displaying a product and fainting with rapture all at the same moment.

And they are shocked by *Flaming Creatures* and have called it obscene. After a great deal of consideration I have realized that I have always been shocked by the sex fantasies for attaining a joyful fulfillment of the drives toward love and union. Of course when the quester after ecstasy finds realistic love the sex fantasies are put aside and forgotten. They should not be regretted when realistic love is attained for when, in the days of their efflorescence, they performed many marvelous functions, they might have masked the sad realities of the inability to love, the burning center of unique creativity from whence flights of poetry and wonder may have flown, from whence sparks of sadness and wit may have been struck, and helped the not quite beautiful to flare into painful beauty . . .

As with much of the previously unpublished writing included here, the preceding essay was transcribed from an unpaginated longhand draft found in the archives left by Jack Smith at the time of his death in 1989. It appears to have been written around 1964, following the seizure of *Flaming Creatures*. A folded sheet of typing paper serving as an envelope was found with the manuscript. It bears a dateless, cancelled stamp commemorating West Virginia's statehood centennial, 1863 – 1963 and is addressed to underground filmmaker and early Warhol superstar Naomi Levine. For purposes of reference, the text is indexed by its introductory words. (E.L.)

LOBOTOMY IN
LOBSTERLAND

JACK SMITH

◯ What kind of baboon sperm is ex

This police crap is a recent thing — there was no such thing as police — armed and numerous as cockroaches — at the time of the writing of the constitution —
— the ever multiplying police + their concomittant of the criminal as the one who gets caught. The police who makes up the law minute by minute — who by this time is confused with the law in the minds of most — the police who frame the ~~charge a~~ and word the charge against one — which is repeated by the judge to the jury in his instructions to them — The Policeman who

O what kind of baboon sperm is exchanged among the populace that creates generations and generations of creatures chained to a bed? O Creator, can monsters exist in the eyes of Him who alone knows how they were created – why they were created and how they might have avoided such a fate? What system that supports in impunity rats, who complain of and turn in their fellows instead of working out their problems themselves? The rat, able to climb straight up, able to crawl anywhere, which *sneaks* its food, which has no control over its rectum – which lives in filth and has a receding chin. The true rat is one who (as well as informs) holds out to the others a slice of white bread (which to rats is like angel cake) in the match tray beneath the burners of a stove while the others are dropping dead of rat poison – and runs away in panic if startled. And who, to support himself turns to the occupation of FEDERAL NARCO.

Rehearsal for the
Destruction of Atlantis –
A Dream Weapon Ritual

These are times when even a masochist must cry out. As Commissioner Gordon remarked at the last meeting of the Orchid Foundation in Gotham City, "How can young American artists keep abreast of the demands of psychedelic art for increasingly elaborate, expensive electronic equipment and at the same time take part in endless jail benefits that do really benefit nobody but jails?" However, these benefits are necessary to pay for and rescue people from the fantastic and irrational legal machinery that has encrusted itself around the growing use of marijuana by people who need, as mankind always has needed, and now more than ever, some relief from the pressure of the world, now become a police state, and who prefer marijuana, a benign herb that grows out of the ground by itself, apparently with god's permission but not the court's, to alcohol which is in startling contrast a most unnaturally distilled, artfully bottled, and cunningly distributed decoction.

Yet who is so lobotomized as to not be able to see the hypocrisy of what it can possibly be that would make the use of the one in accordance with our constitution and the other not?

Besides which there bulks voluminously and ludicrously a study in anomaly, a government misclassification – alcohol is a narcotic and pot is not. Thus we are in the words of Mary Baker Eddy, straining out gnats and swallowing camels.

Marijuana puffing tho is a quick and easy source of frightened revenues to a jurisprudence of sophistry and its handmaiden a police agency which has assumed, in arming itself against now vanished mad dog crime, a mad dog character itself and in lieu of an adversary worthy of itself has turned upon the public – which process necessitates that more and more matters that affect public life be declared criminal in order to contain insurrection against the Lobster.

But this is a process opposite to the one good government ideally should take – that is to gradually diminish and hopefully disappear. A law must be a true reflection of the thinking of the people on the matter it deals with but what has been overlooked tho, is that to make the use of marijuana criminal is obviously not the will of the people. The situation is ethically ridiculous as well as numerically since in this matter combined with all others of current social change that we face today, creates a population of criminals battened on by the various elite various agencies.

Thus, the ballroom of the Broadway Central Hotel on the night of August the 11th, 1965 was the scene of a benefit program of readings of poetry and underground movies for the purpose of raising lawyer/court funds for Dale Wilbourn and Jack Martin who faced imprisonment on a marijuana entrapment case, since dismissed, wherein Ray Cutler, a man who has many charges hanging over him and who has been frequently used by narcotics agents to inform on his ex-friends (he was flown to Texas to testify against Timothy Leary that he had seen him smoking marijuana at a Village party).

It was a late summer night, narcotic night to overstimulate Narcos and suffuse their brains with lurid imaginations. A perfect lobster moon, full and orange, hung low in the horizon. A night that was to produce a sort of Boston Tea Party to the lonesome latter years and demonstrate what can happen when a law no longer reflects the will and conscience of the people – fantasia, capriccios, the ridiculous! That night of the Lobster-moon charade of the Narco goon squad the potted palms of the Broadway Central ballroom bristled and spawned strange coconuts. Rejected and bitter, frustrated in their attempts to persuade Jack Martin to aid in setting up Allen Ginsberg, and overstimulated by the full moon and not inconceivably drunk, in disguise, and without warrants, they were drawn to the Broadway Central Hotel. They were aware that this was to be an "Abolition of Jails" benefit because upon the last occasion they had Martin in custody they had searched him and found the design of the tickets upon him.

IN THE GRIP OF THE LOBSTER!
The Broadway Central-Lawless Palazzo! Here is re-staged annually for newspaper reporters and photographers the shooting of Jay Gould on the stairway by the husband of his mistress as was John F. Kennedy by the Lobster. The Broadway Central! Once noted by Herman Melville. Its ballroom not always the haunt of lobsters. Its afternoon now spent as the setting for barmitzvahs and 0 now so recently raided!

Assorted Narcos led by their group leader Ike _____ were in fact there to see if they might seek some opportunity to rearrest Martin who they knew to be outspoken and who they, knowing it was to be an abolition of jails benefit, expected would probably describe his experience with them. And that, or something else that might happen, or be caused to happen, would constitute enough of a basis for his rearrest to their thinking and I use the word advisedly. They were protecting themselves – of course – they were anticipating some crime that would not even pertain to narcotics directly but that could involve anticipated unrestrained speech. They were disguised – they altered their appearance in such a way as to appear as other than narcotics agents but in their attempt to blend in with the beats who were actually dressed elegantly and conservatively, unwillingly created outlandish caricatures of moldy 1940's saloon-rioting waterfront scum of Flatulandia in pasty short sleeve Hawaiian sport shirts. They threw the moulds away after they made these cupcakes.

I arrived at the ballroom of the Broadway Central that night at 7:30. Since we were showing films I hung an improvised screen on the stage. Then I sat down in the side of the front row, and at 8:00 Jack Martin, partly reading from notes, made a speech which I imperfectly apprehended due to his vehemence and a bad p.a. system.

Piero Heliczer, a poet, who was to read his own work interrupted to announce that unless certain creatures who had crashed into the ballroom without paying the admission left immediately the program would not continue. Jack Martin resumed his address to reveal that Federal Narcotics Agents had attempted to induce him to aid them in entrapping Allen Ginsberg, the poet, which he had refused to do. Suddenly, grotesquely, there were 3 or 4 men of remarkably low aspect, sweating and panting clad in Hawaiian sport shirts, dancing around Martin and pulling and hauling at him.

HAIL O LOBSTER

The ballroom audience of by then 200 persons was thrown into pandemonium. Women were screaming and fighting broke out. Jack Martin was seized by a number of these louts, who did not identify themselves, who indeed had altered their identities as Federal Narcotics agents and whom I assumed were baboons and who dragged Jack bodily and violently thru the now panicked crowd. I followed the crowd as it spilled out into the sidewalk. I saw struggling. I heard Piero Heliczer's cries of pain as he was dragged along with his arm being twisted behind him. I saw one of the creatures in Hawaiian shirts skipping along behind the struggling group – I caught a glimpse of his face – he was smiling radiantly at Piero's cries of pain. I struck him and was instantly knocked to the sidewalk and sat upon by a gargantuan Jon Hall. Jon Hall's all. Since then my life has become a protracted struggle to remain out of jail – wasteful of money and disruptive of work.

Thru the delirium of a mangled court trial I REALIZE too late that if our lawyer had thought of complaining to the Civilian Review Board about the beating I received at the station house, where we were first taken, at the hands of a Detective Imp, that that might have saved our case; that our lawyer whom we found, too late, had no special convictions of his own involved in our behalf and indeed who makes his living at the way things are and all of whose interests lie in keeping them that way was unable to convince a jury of 12 elderly senior office-clerk types that the agents hadn't properly identified themselves and were not there in some undirected way in the line of their duties. That they, being narcotics agents, could not be there other than being about their narcotics duties, since they, in analogy, being clerks mostly could only be employed with their clerk duties. Nevertheless, presumably out of gallantry, Irene Nolan, the only girl of the 4 arrested, against whom the charge, assaulting Federal Narcotics Agents, was identical was found innocent.

But that is what would be unbearable, to be found innocent by these courts. I see life being crushed by the courts as casually as a car crushes debris beneath its wheels pulling away from the curb. I see people wandering around absent-mindedly trying to recall the court details of their lives through streets littered with wreckage from the aftermath of an explosion crushed into a spectacular heap by departing juggernauts spread out on the sidewalk as though it were the unglued surface of life for passers by to pick their way through who can not know what has been lost in court. The lost love of our courts.

SWAN LAKE – AFTER ATLANTIS

The deserted court house at Swan Lake
Pussys erupting in air
Let's put on a play with words
It will be in a court house
We'll invite the public

How many thousands can we be sure of . . .
Are felt to be gambled Safely Upon
First witness (in black) – O dile . . .
O for love of her.

PLAYED BY
MARIO MONTEZ
although not the true ideal.
And not under Oath as would we all
If we knew what we were doing
As we do of course, All!!!!
Arise Pasties of Lotusland
Happiness destroyed Atlantis
Anarchy in Lobsterland!
Atlantis needs Anarchy.
Life can be lost in court.
A perfect Swan Lake of wrecked lives left demented by their moment in court.
Never mind the life lost in the electric chairs
Life can be lost in court
Anything is lost which goes to court,
not because right or wrong are won or lost but
where decisions are made – and what are the only
considerations that ever entered into any decision that any human was ever in or knows of – economic pressures.

Where good and evil in black and white costumes are paraded endlessly seeming always to be on some delicate balance like tired tightrope walkers, truth forever teetering breathlessly. And who goes there deserves what he gets because he has already been too guilty of confusing life with chance. Am I right or wrong is not only not a thing to be speculated upon in public but doesn't matter since good and evil are too impacted with the substance of life to be separated and judged and can only have dignity if it never crosses over the threshold of a court house, which should be as naturally loathsome as stockyards, but resists with what ever means may be available and unlimited by the imagination, to physically entering a court house and no longer gathering in court as in a slaughtering hall of prejudged, already stale, delicate economic pressures when we are perfectly able to feel that we are being turned into rats deserting a sinking ship by what is going on in Vietnam anyway.

On August 11, 1965, Smith participated in a protest held at the ballroom of the old Broadway Central Hotel. The Smith-titled event, "Grass Busts of the Brassiere World," was convened in support of the abolition of jails, and in support of Dale Wilbourn and Jack Martin, men who faced imprisonment on an entrapment case. Martin, who had been arrested for possession of marijuana on July 23, protested specifically against the legality of a law enforcement agency to bargain with the accused, exchanging leniency for information. Specifically, Martin was to set up Allen Ginsberg for a narcotics bust. About 200 people assembled, and Martin gave a short speech calling for an opening of the books, an investigation and full disclosure of the bargaining practice. Smith wrote a recollection by way of protest of the conduct of undercover agents during the rally.

In a three-page statement dated May 25, 1966, Ginsberg writes that he did not know Martin prior to his arrest, but praised his speech at the Broadway Central Hotel as sensible, "passionate short prose, and charmingly stands in authentic patriotic Tradition with dear Tom Paine.... The speech is political. The tableau of such speech ending with an attack on his person by agents of the very bureaucracy he was criticizing is one of classic familiar injustice." He asks the listener/reader to consider the "quality of person of the other defendants." District Attorney Bartel, requesting high bail for Smith, referred to him as "an unemployed filmmaker," ". . . stuck with a broken leg in his loft in New York & preoccupied with his material completing his editing of a new film . . . must now scrape money together for bail as consequence of being categorized as 'unemployed filmmaker' by a Harvard Graduate government attorney the newspapers of the day proclaim the appropriation of hundreds of thousands of dollars for a National Arts Committee to subsidize the 'arts.' " He refers to Heliczer, and says that the poet "for once, took unwonted physical action to defend principles of privacy and speech and courtesy – honor, even, since he was defending his lady who was defending hero Martin bullied on the sidewalk by agents of the Government. Now Mr. Heliczer's money and anxiety goes to bail, jail, legal appeal, trips to the American Civil Liberties Union – trapped in a Kafkian network of unjust law and administration of such law . . . (Remember, the officers had no warrant to arrest Mr. Martin! Nor any but flabby excuse! Simply *illegal!*)"

Ginsberg goes on to say that his role was brought out by Martin in court, "safeguarding me – perhaps – from future harassment or entrapment by my own government. Neither Judge or Jury nor Prosecutor heard of me as other than 'a film maker who made an underground movie named *Blow Job*. Unfortunately, I wasn't a participant in Andy Warhol's movie, and I am actually a poet sufficiently respectable to be a Guggenheim Fellow . . . but I would like to make the point that the court, jury and all, could have no sense of the enormity of the damage attempted on the artistic community – myself a filmmaker." He concludes, "We are assailed on every side by rancor and hostility multiplied billionfold megaphoned into our senses by electronic media, till the populace has lost contact with its own meaty Self. We are not born for this, and we will destroy ourselves if it continues." (E.L.)

REHEARSAL FOR

THE DESTRUCTION

ATLANTIS

REHEARSAL FOR THE DESTRUCTION OF ATLANTIS

A Dream Weapon Ritual by Jack Smith

Dedicated to Irving Rosenthal

Presented at the Film-Makers' Cinematheque on November 7th and 8th, 1965

with a cast that included the following players:

John Vaccaro – The Lobster
Mario Montez – dancer
Jeanne Phillips – Mehboubeh
Jack Smith – dancer
Joel Markman – dancer
Tally Brown – Siamese twin – 1st nite
Julie Garfield – Siamese twin – 1st nite
Barbara Rubin – Siamese twin – 2nd nite
Babette Long – Siamese twin – 2nd nite
Franklin Crowley – NARCO
Mark Safron – NARCO
Tosh Carillo – NARCO
Will Gay – NARCO

Special assistance:
Tosh Carillo – design
David Gurin – material for Vietnam tape

Time: the present.
Place: Atlantis . . . A child's vegetable garden of foreign policy cadavers.

The audience files in blindfolded. Their files are taken from them and the usherettes (very tough Lesbians) (in matron uniforms) see that all blindfolds are in place. A man in the audience objects to his blindfold. He is roughly cuffed and manhandled by the usherettes into submission to the bandage. Chloroform could be used.
The house lights and music dim.
The curtains remain closed.

Over the p.a. a mad voice:

"You are to imagine that you are a wino. This afternoon you were over-come by a fit of drowsiness and sun – baking and half asleep. Your skin feels oily. Your socks are clammy. Your head feels like a coconut – your eyes like sore rectums. You are uncomfortably hot but you lay entirely motionless. A police wino wagon drives up and suddenly, rudely you are prodded by a night-stick. You are dragged to your feet. You had a bottle in your pocket which was deliberately smashed by the night-stick. All the way to the station you have to sit on a pocketful of broken glass with a wet pant leg. You are driven to a skyscraper prison. It is disguised to look like an ordinary skyscraper. As the wagon approaches it you perceive beneath screens, bars at all the windows. The walls have widely spaced stripes of dark and light which make it look even more like a prison. Whether by accident or design or both.

Inside your belongings are checked and you are ordered to get naked. Then you are herded through a foot-bath for athlete's foot. Then you are made to take a bath against your will and sprayed with D.D.T. Then you are kept in a cell for a couple of days – and then – after standing in line to be given back your possessions – you are released. On your way out you observe Wino Wagons passing to and fro in the streets – bringing other winos into the prison, all of which is no doubt to provide a flexible means of keeping the number of prisoners in the building at a constant level.

This is your tiny wino role in the perfect operation of the threat under which we live. All because you have no ego, are overly sentimental about your mother – but thus the necessary punishment for having prisons is diffused among the population. O what kind of baboon sperm is exchanged among the populace that creates generations and generations of creatures chained to a bed. O creator! can monsters exist in the eyes of Him who alone knows how they were created – why they were created and how they might have avoided such a fate! That maintains a system that supports in impunity rats who complain of and turn in their fellows instead of working out ones problems oneself. The RAT, able to climb straight up, able to crawl anywhere, which *sneaks* its food, which has no control over its rectum – which lives in filth and has a receding chin – the true rat is one which (as well as informs) holds out on the others a slice of white bread (which to rats is like angel food cake) in the match tray beneath the burners of a stove while the others are dropping dead of rat poison – and runs away in panic if startled. And who, to support himself turns to the occupation of FEDERAL NARCO!"

(Curtain slowly, silently opens to reveal the siamese (North and South) twin queen of Atlantis. (Vietnam))

Twins: (in unison) "Take off your blindfolds now, you are in Atlantis!"

One to the other: "O let us smoke some of the marijuana that grows so abundantly and legally in the many extensive fields and plains here in Atlantis!"

Other twin says: "O yes indeed it transports me to a magical paradise." Twins call: "Mehboubeh, Mehboubeh – bring the pipe." (Mehboubeh does.) They establish that marijuana grows both in North and South Atlantis & establish which each one is. Mehboubeh leaves stage & they find they need a match – they argue about who should go. They go get matches somewhere. Mehboubeh returns. One strikes the match – it goes out. The other says: "You think you know how to strike a match. You think that simply by scraping a match across some sandpaper you can light a match. Well, you're wrong! What do *you* know of the centuries of science of progress, of the contributions of Madame Curie, Thomas Edison, Edouard Manet, Lewis Stone or Edward Arnold. Of the Andrews Sisters or Maria Montez! Of Travis Banton or Van Nest Polglase!"[1] (Mehboubeh goes on her knees trembling.) U.S. Federal Narcos in rat masks lurk about in background in order artificially to surround the smoking of a benign herb with all the aura of illegality established with criminal evidence collected. For future purposes . . .

A procession of Dancers in white come in – the lead dancer carries a matchbook and chants: "As windmills upon the earth turn and turn again – so upon the sea sails fill and fulfill while the mysteries of the winds blow ever as they list. Rabbinical lore whispers betimes of wind angels that die as soon as born and it is said old hags still sell winds on knotted strings to superstitious sailors on wharves of Norway!" (Match is struck & pipe lit) (they puff happily – Mehboubeh enters with a tape recorder – she explains:)

Mehboubeh: "Everybody in the U.S.A. wants to manufacture and buy tape recorders but no one wants to repair them."

Twin: "But the manufacturers must be incredibly wealthy – what do they do with their money?"

(Debut Detroit Style tape begins, dancers come on stage and film is projected over them for a production number illustrating the tawdry waste of wealthy mfgrs.)

(During the prod. no. the two narcos in rat masks are on stage spying.)

Twins: (to Mehboubeh) "What kind of Moon is it tonight?"

(Mehboubeh goes out – comes back – says:) "The moon is full, Mistress." (She goes back out and returns with the moon held as a platter & goes past twins to hang it up. As she passes them – they pick a paper off the moon – (*National Enquirer* – headline: Mother Kills Twin So Other May Live).

The next event: the twins become involved in a fantastic quarrel over who should get the arm of the armchair which has only one arm. They end by dragging it clumsily off stage.

The Lobster enters with gigantic salad fork and spoon and crepe paper lettuce leaves. He arranges the lettuce leaves around the base of the throne platform reciting a moon poem. Now the platform will be used as an operating table. After the moon poem the Vietnam tape commences to play. [2]

As Vietnam tape begins the twins enter bickering carrying pot pipe & newspaper. The Rat-narcos observe the pot pipe with magnifying glass and seize one of the twins. The other twin draws her space gun and covers her other half as the twin is dragged to operating table. They are severed with an electric circular saw. One dies right away. The other, the puppet, South-Atlantis lives a little while but expires in the lobster's arms, still holding the gun. (During operation Mario Montez dances around operating table to music of *Swan Lake*.)

The Lobster, in a daze, puts lettuce leaves over the bodies & tries to cover them. The dancers, smiling like chorus girls come out one by one with the vegetables and place them on top of the littered operating table. The tape recorder and every thing else in sight are piled in his arms and smoke erupts from top of platform as from a volcano, rises around the Lobster and obscures the stage, then the theater as the Lobster screams at audience: "Put back your blindfolds – then don't – I don't care – get out I don't need you – Get out of my dressing room – OUT!"

Film Culture #40 (Spring 1966)

Smith presented *Rehearsal for the Destruction of Atlantis* on November 7 and 8, 1965, at the Astor Film-Makers' Cinematheque venue as part of the New Cinema Festival of "Expanded Cinema" organized by Jonas Mekas. In the *Village Voice* (11/18/65), Mekas described the piece as "an orgy of costumes, suppressed and open violence, and color. The center of the piece was a huge red lobster, a masterpiece creation of costume and character." According to Mekas, *Rehearsal for the Destruction of Atlantis* "was loose and relied on chance, on coincidences, on conglomerations." Other participants in the festival included Stan Vanderbeek, Nam June Paik, Claes Oldenburg, Robert Rauschenberg, La Monte Young, Marion Zazeela, and Angus MacLise.

In addition to the typescript essay reprinted here and as "Part Two" in *Historical Treasures*, the

Jack Smith Archive contains a second, shorter typescript titled "Lobster Moon over the Broadway Central." A longhand draft anticipates the final typescript, and in its roughly fifteen pages, Smith considers other titles, among them "Contempt of Court," "Mortal Abhorrance of Court," "Lobster Moon," "The Revenge of the Lobster," "The Raided Ballroom," and "Strange Case of the Invaded Ballroom." (E.L.)

1. Travis Banton gained a reputation for designing Marlene Dietrich's daring costumes in her Paramount films with Josef von Sternberg. Art director Van Nest Polglase created the elegant art deco sets for RKO's Astaire-Rogers movies, among many other films. (J.H.)

2. In a November 1978 interview with the coeditor, Smith described the tape, made by political activist David Gurin, as a reading of "some newspaper clippings of little-known information on Vietnam – a surprise then but it wouldn't be a surprise now." (J.H.)

Ammonia Pits of Atlantis:
Evil in the Art World
or
WALTER VERSUS THE GIANT KNICK KNACKS

In Staten Island recently a housing development was condemned to be destroyed though at the time of condemnation, the buildings were under construction. There were water leaks, cracked foundations, and faulty plumbing that must have been pretty disgusting. And upon another, more gilded occasion, a rehearsal at the new Met of its opening opera, *Anthony and Cleopatra*, a huge pyramid, designed to open, close over Cleopatra, travel toward the backstage, and melt from view did actually open and clamp over its prey but stalled mid-stage in its voyage imprisoning, for a time, Leontyne Price, the Cleopatra of the new American opera while workmen toiled to shift the pyramid back onto its hydraulic carrier and to repair the snapped cable pulling it. But the curse of cretinism falls most heavily upon the poor parts of the city, poor people are sticking their fingers into the piecrust-like formations that occur when many layers of bad paint buckle away from the plaster and puff out, releasing through the sores endless torrents of fine, powdery black excrescence and roach eggcase crumblings from the entire decaying building. The times are the times they are, spectacularly bad times comparable only to the last days of Rome, Pompeii, or Atlantis, and now that we do in fact have a steaming police Atlantis where the populace walks about in the streets demolished into settings for assassination, haunted by slowly crawling patrol cars and police bristling in every dark doorway like roaches, glad not to be in jail, and never aware of the real problem – a staggering social problem, the only social problem in fact, inflicted by courts become Orchid Foundations supported by the police, made to feel like cockroaches deserting a sinking continent where no one is more confused than the roaches themselves who think we are inviting them to live in our houses behind some pasty crust or other, and where our schools are busily erasing the history of the recent past by presenting ancient history as history. Except, apparently, in Art.

Things can't be recent enough in the art world, where if an artist doesn't exploit his style soon enough to suit another artist it may very well be taken over by anyone who may feel that it properly belongs to whoever can rush it into the popular magazines first. In fact there is an artificial frenzy of intensity created in the search for artists to feed into the moronic pages of the magazines. Walter de Maria's sculpture, because of its remarkable austerity has until lately when a chunk of him was fed into the ammonia pits of Atlantis to baboon chatter been proof against the feathered sharks of the art world. Its influence has, rather, been felt benignly in the lives of his friends with surprising urgency and with clarity because his work is concerned with structure. The purity of Walter's life and work does not belie the fact that he has been building all his life, beginning with his boxes, basically, as boxes are basic to architecture, as surely as sculpture is basic to architecture.

Except for the work of Antoine Pevsner, I care even less for modern sculpture than I do for the idea of Modern Art replacing Art. The importance of sculpture is the importance we give it by the apparent deference of Christianity to human values at the expense of objects, things. But Christianity actually is a framework for explaining matter, since we know very well where people come from. Consequently when we adore someone we make an object of him – or tiny sculptures. This is a misapplication of sculpture, though, since Christian ideas don't work very well for humans, except for those engaged in the business of Courts, and when it was realized, about the time of Heidegger, that they were turning us into vampires the figure was removed, leaving only the cross which remained a true frame of reference for humans since the change in Christianity was even more superficial and even less true. This alteration, however, angered the plaster manufacturers who started the Church in the first place, so sculpture became a blob, everyone decided God was dead and turned, en masse, to dry-cleaning fetishism, and the object became more and more plastered in response to the demands of the liquor manufacturers and their hench-maidens, the courts. Then God got sore and accusing man's best works of being filthy rags in his sight, flounced off to hide from the splattering plaster as man went on to build himself ever more stately mansions with pastry tubes.

Walter de Maria is a sculptor in a way that an idea of sculpture is needed to counteract the plaster idea of sculpture and by being a non plaster sculptor extends his non plaster approach to architecture by association by his architectonic approach to a plaster oriented art and a plaster smothered architecture and thereby achieves the fantastic significance of his art.

His work is endlessly vital and vibrant because it bears a non-relationship to plaster art and to an architecture which has become merely scaffolding to support our precious plaster architecture long since vacated by structure and crumbling at varyingly rapid rates on construction sites, onstage at the new Met and within the rooms in which we live, where the plaster of religion, the cement of the courts, and their extension in art, icing, meet on our very piecrust walls behind which the materials of building, wood, metal, brick, stone, whatever are covered over, buried, lost behind the effortless, quick, automatic smooth success of a coat of plaster – become an eggshell adored by the MOMA as Nature's Perfect Package and so perfect for the perfect preservation of our ladybird motherhood and perfect police protection from anything whatsoever even though in reality the egg was rotten a long time in 1910.

What is this work of Walter de Maria's that places him so firmly on the side of structure? The principle is as simple as the box, in fact, is the box. His first sculptures were just that – bafflingly simple boxes. I first apprehended them as an extensive vaginal reference but his recent high energy bars provide a phallic joke just as appropriate to a structural construction of his art. The early boxes were wood – now, although he works in stainless steel and zinc due to a fortuitous conjunction with the ideas and sponsorship of Robert Scull, the principle has remained exactly the same and will remain the same tho his sculptures are dropped on the floor, a contingency fraught with potential effluvium for the ageless plaster eggshell. Walter has lived with his artistic principles all his thinking life, suffered with their fixity, and worried over their purity all his building life. And Walter has been building all his life.

I've known him only four years but I would make a guess of intuition that he has been building his principles since about the age of six. I remember that there was a time in my boyhood about 6 - 11 when boxes, at first wooden, then cardboard, meant all to me. I lived to crawl into boxes – very large clean cardboard boxes being the most glorious. Except for wearing them out I didn't alter them but was happy to just sit inside them. That may have the only happiness I knew; I do definitely remember that it was deep and true happiness. Soon after that, all the plaster icing of Hollywood was to inundate my sensibilities and set obstacles to artistic development, such as, social problems are due to lack of love, and a Belasco naturalism arrested, paralysed, plastered, tinted, and embalmed forever at a florid peak of wealthy marination, such as I will have to chip at all my life for the sake of my soul, as, to some extent or other, do we all.

For these reasons – because Walter de Maria is all we have to counteract the loss of structure in our time, and everything supported by structure, such as gaiety, because he is an artist with his eye on no other artist, because he isn't an artist whose life can be chopped into by the galleries one day and be used up the next (to be obliged to find a new style – from somewhere – the next, in order to exist) because he places sculpture in its proper relation to architecture, in miniature & in advance, because his sculpture is not sculpture – because sculpture has discredited itself by becoming giant knick-knacks, and yet is witty, and because it is beautiful because it is simple, and also because Walter has poured his life into it, I suggest you see his show at the Cordier-Ekstrom gallery before it closes on Saturday Dec. the 3rd.[1]

It's too bad you missed it.
Walter against the roaches of various kinds in 1000 ways.

THIS IS AN ESSAY

This essay, clearly intended for publication, was written on the occasion of a Walter de Maria exhibition at the Cordier-Ekstrom Gallery, New York City, November/December 1966. The Jack Smith Archive of the Plaster Foundation includes a handwritten draft, an annotated typescript, and a fair copy. The text was apparently never published, and Mr. de Maria declines comment. (E.L.)

1. A description of the de Maria exhibition may be found in Michael Benedikt's "Sculpture as Architecture: New York Letter, 1966 – 67" (included in Gregory Battcock's 1968 *Minimal Art: A Critical Anthology*).

> The show's centerpiece was a black ziggurat, with
> many dozens of tiny steps: at the very top, head-
> high, was a shiny vinyl chair, with chrome frame.
> It was like a throne. A theatrical tension entered
> through the fact that the feet of the chair were at
> the corner-tips of the base upon which it stood . . .

The writer deems de Maria's work only "*relatively* Minimal," attributing the artist's theatricality to his association with Happenings by Claes Oldenburg and Robert Whitman.

Benedikt further notes a series of framed drawings, each a single, "shakily lettered" word evoking some aspect of the natural landscape. "The balance of the show," he concludes,

> consisted of a series of rather Duchampian follies
> involving small chromed objects – mostly in the shape
> of hollowed-out, cheeseboxlike shapes. One of these
> was in the shape of a Christian cross, and had a ball
> in it, evoking both piety and the pinball-machine.
> The largest of all consisted of two long rows of
> chromed brick shapes. From the top of each, three
> chromed poles protruded, some round, some hexagonal,
> some high, some low, in unpredictable patterns. One
> walked into De Maria's show through them, as if down
> a long avenue of sphinxes reinterpreted.
> (J.H.)

TABOO OF JINGOLA

There is a living feeling about the *Reefer Madness* program at the Elgin these recent midnights which is the closest I've seen to the wonderful orgasmiatic explosion that was the at the Charles Theatre in, what was it? – 1960 – 61? – and which was probably the golden age of that sort of thing in movies for those who remember it. [1]

Reefer Madness is a short film – 30, maybe 45 minutes. It is a dynamite film so no other feature is needed. Hence it can be best set off by other shorter features and an interesting principle discovered and a flawless frontier opened up. The Elgin midnights don't really compare – what could? The Charles screenings were wide open. People brought in their own films and saw them on the huge Charles screen – a truly surrealistic experience – to see those films on that huge Hollywood screen – and they looked damn good. All the ingredients are there at the Elgin – the scum of Bagdad audience with the yelling of witticisms, sound effects, booing, cheering, etc., pathetically eager and straining to encourage the screen to give the hallucinations they know very well are locked up in the movie business – maybe even a bargain – a burst of generosity in these stingy times.

If there ever could be such a thing as giving (as opposed to careful measuring out), the logical place to begin is in film exhibition. The rental of the extra films it would take to make a super-program could easily be covered by the full houses they would create. And so movies could easily demonstrate that sharing might be so much better as business than the eternal competition that makes life so dreary. I knew a theatre owner who maintained a high price policy because he didn't want too many people in the theatre messing it up. (That theatre owner has since gone out of business.) It's really a psychological problem – what has to be surmounted is the convention of the idea of competition that is all we have known since this country fell on its knees before the tin promise of the assembly line and the historically related concept of unlimited profit.

This may have been good business for a very few but brutalizing for most people, and I think a counter-idea is behind the riotous cheering of audiences for any program – in films, music, or theatre – that offers or seems to offer an un-measured-out program. Not that the *Reefer* program at the Elgin doesn't qualitatively measure up to such expectations. It is a wonderful film that should be seen by anybody in film or the arts. It is fertile by reason of the primitiveness of its expression. The work of the primitive or naive artist is always fertile for the study of other artists – if only because it breaks through, to one extent or another, the restrictions to the imagination of naturalism.

Marijuana, not more a drug than consumerism and much less hypnotic than landlordism, is in fact an herb which, like every other herb, has its own beneficial property for humans – and *Reefer Madness* comes by its marvelous appeal dishonestly – but therein lies the artistic lesson the film has for us. It depicts, with all the conviction of a medium soaked in naturalism, the disintegration of its character – especially the leading man – who turns in the most wonderful ham performance I have ever seen in a movie. He is given every opportunity to disintegrate to the point of gilded splendor. No sooner is one joint greedily puffed than another is lighted from it with trembling hand and stuck in the quivering visage – all blear and with eyes popping – a pothead's dream come true.

So we see at full strength the magic of the movies heightened by a sympathetic art style – the untrue made true – what is not made to be. If this can be done anything can be done, can be said – liberation. The same is true tho in less marvelous degree of the other film of the program the night I saw it – only because of not having the blessing of the actor in *Reefer* (whose name I wasn't watching for because the credits preceded the films). This was a trumped-up depiction of the horrendousness of the devil-weed upon the poor people of Cairo made by the Egyptian government.

Then there was a short film called *The Dream of a Rarebit Fiend* included as thematic extension. It might have worked with sound. And of course the Betty Boop cartoon that expanded the feeling of nut hilarity of the evening very nicely. Then it was over. Just short of a truly great stroke of showmanship.

I wondered how much more it would have cost to have retained the opium eater short with Vincent Price I'd noticed had been on the program when it was at the Garrick. Or how much more would it have cost to include any other color short subject or to round out the program and send hundreds of people out of the theatre really happy and with that full feeling – and satisfy that hope in audiences that miraculously seems to never die. It is too simplistic to say that the audience makes the theatre. They have created theatres where there has been any promise – even if false – so eager is the audience for spontaneous theatre that a Jonas Mekas, more a Rona Barrett than a Savonarola but less a guru than a praying mantis, was easily able to go from co-op to pawnshop to anthology in 10 easy years.

The Charles Theatre (for which *Flaming Creatures* incidentally, was specifically made) unfortunately had its golden age ended when the ecstasy got out of hand and it became difficult to collect admissions because of the confusion of film-makers and audience. When financial realities intruded on the scene, the management began to measure out carefully the programs and collapsed shortly thereafter.

In spite of these examples, I can – as can any audience – easily imagine a situation where there would be more for everybody through a process whereby we share in some way as consummately as competition is carried out. The *Reefer* multiple unit programs, insofar as they approach such economics, are distinguished and imaginative theatre and are almost as hip as their audiences.

The Village Voice (December 21, 1972)

1. The Charles Theater, a 700-seat movie house on Avenue B, between 11th and 12th Streets, was run by a pair of young film buffs – Walter Langsford and Ed Stein – from late 1961

through the following Summer. In the winter of 1961 – 62, at the suggestion of guest programmer Jonas Mekas, the theater began hosting monthly open screenings to which admission was ninety-five cents or one film. These culminated with a single grand Filmmakers Festival in July 1962 around the time Smith began filming *Flaming Creatures* on the roof of another Lower East Side moviehouse, the Windsor, which Langsford and Stein were hoping (in vain) to reopen.

A low-budget exploitation film, released in 1940 at the height of Federal Drug Commissioner Henry J. Anslinger's campaign against the "killer weed," *Reefer Madness* (a/k/a *The Burning Question* a/k/a *Tell Your Children* a/k/a *Doped Youth*) is at once sanctimonious and salacious. When a group of smalltown high-school kids take to smoking marijuana rather than playing tennis, the results are hit-and-run driving, promiscuous sex, attempted rape, incurable madness, multiple murder, and eventual suicide. As the most dissolute hophead in the film, an actor named David O'Brien gives one of the broad portrayals of mental illness ever committed to celluloid.

Reefer Madness was directed by Louis Gasnier who, after discovering comedian Max Linder, emigrated from France to Hollywood to direct the serial *The Perils of Pauline* and remained to make 33 silent features. (As his English evidently left something to be desired, Gasnier had an erratic post-sound career that, in fact, ended the year after *Reefer Madness* was released.) The movie had lain forgotten for three decades when Keith Stroup, head of the National Organization for the Reform of Marijuana Laws (NORML), discovered it in the Library of Congress film archive and, because the film was in the public domain, purchased a print (for $297) which he immediately put to work: *Reefer Madness* had its first revival at a midnight NORML benefit at the St. Marks Theater in May 1972 and, an instant hit, went on to play midnight shows in New York and California for the remainder of the year. (J.H.)

Armoured Real Estate hatchet woman on wheels

UNCLE FISHOOK AND THE SACRED
BABY POO POO OF ART

Sylvére Lotringer: *How did you get the idea to make* Flaming Creatures?

Jack Smith: I started making a comedy about everything that I thought was funny. And it *was* funny. The first audiences were laughing from the beginning all the way through. But then *that writing* started – and it became a sex thing. It turned the movie into a magazine sex issue. It was fed to the magazines. Lesbian writers were finding purple titillations. Then it fertilized Hollywood. Wonderful. When they got through licking their chops over the movie there was no more laughter. There was dead silence in the auditorium. The film was practically used to destroy me.

L: *Wasn't there a trial?*
S: There was a trial and I lost. Uncle Jonas' lawyers were doing the trial, and at some point it was dropped. And if a case is dropped, it can't be appealed. Now the movie is permanently illegal in New York.

L: *Can't it be shown in some places, under certain conditions?*
S: Uncle Fishook was showing it at his mausoleum, but that's because no one has complained. . . . It would be inconvenient to have anybody complain. But when he needed a complaint, there was a complaint. At one time it was fashionable to have a work of art in the courts. All the mileage gotten out of Miller's books. . . . And Uncle Fishook wanted to have something in court at the time, it being so fashionable. The publicity. It was another way by which he could be made to look like a saint, to be in the position of defending something when he was really kicking it to death. So he would give screenings of *Creatures* and making speeches, defying the police to bust the film. Which they did. And then there was the trial . . . I don't know what the lawyers were doing. I wasn't even permitted to be in the court. I walked into the courtroom and my lawyer said, "Go out of the courtroom," and I said, "Why?" – "because the judge is upset by too many men with beards." I was ordered to leave by the

marshmallow lawyer that Uncle Mekas had. So I couldn't even see the trial. You know: it goes on and on.

L: *I must say that when I saw the film at the Cinématheque, people were laughing their heads off.*
S: Mumble, mumble. It inflated Uncle Fishook; it made his career; I ended up supporting him. He's been doing my travelling for 15 years. He's been conducting a campaign to dehumanize me in his column. There's just a list of monstrosities. I don't want to start that. . . . So from supporting Uncle Fishook, now we're left years later with nothing. There's nothing anybody can do with their films. *He's* got the original.

L: *You don't have any copy?*
S: I have a miserable beat up inter-negative that's shot. He must have sucked 1,000 copies out of it. It needs to be restored or something.

L: *Why don't you make another film?*
S: I don't want to let somebody go running off with . . . I am. I've already made new films; I have a roomful of films that I've made since then. . . . But there's nothing in the world that I can do with them, because Uncle Fishook has established this pattern of the way film is thought about, and seen, and everything else . . .

L: *Did you actually mean anything through your film?*
S: No, I didn't then. But the meaning has to come out in what is done with the art – is what gives it meaning. The way my movie was used – that was the meaning of the movie.

L: *You mean that meaning comes afterwards?*
S: What you do with it economically is what the meaning is. If it goes to support Uncle Fishook, that's what it means. Movies are always made for an audience. But I didn't make it that way. I was just making it completely for myself. At the time, that seemed like an intellectual experiment. But that point got lost.

L: *But that happens everytime someone wants to make art.*

S: If they weren't making this deliberately pointless art, then it wouldn't happen. . . . And it wouldn't have happened to me if I had been perfect. It wouldn't have been taken up and used by somebody else.

L: *I read recently what Susan Sontag wrote about* Flaming Creatures . . .

S: It showed that she was just as hypnotized by him as I was . . . but by that time I was no longer hypnotized by him and she . . .

L: *She said it didn't mean anything, and that was the strength of the film. I liked that. It's not just that it was comical, but that it makes fun of all sorts of ideas we have, and definitions . . .*

S: Was it being exploited like Hollywood? Uncle Fishook's use of the word *co-op* just drifted past Miss Sontag. . . . And nobody seems to expect anything from that idea. They don't seem to know what a co-op is.

L: *What is it about?*

S: It's a thing that controls all the activities of a certain activity. And then everyone engaged in this is sharing the money.

L: *Is that the way your film was done?*

S: A film co-op sounded like something I wanted to do, to support. I turned over my film to this film co-op. And then it became a grotesque parody of Hollywood. Uncle Fishook was heroic in her review. What was heroic? Taking someone's film away from him . . . Uncle Roachcrust perpetuated the monstrosity of discrediting co-ops. That's why he is a symbol, an Uncle Pawnshop, a symbol of fishook co-ops. The only reason for the pattern of the 2 night screenings he has established is so somebody's film will spend one night in the safe – if you get my meaning.

L: *Didn't you want to destroy your work?*

S: Uncle Fishook says all kinds of fantastic things about me. If anybody that can only comprehend capitalism would look at my behavior and the only conclusion that they could come to was that I was trying to destroy myself.

L: *When capitalism is in fact trying to destroy you?*

S: And he's printed things like that in his column. Once he printed that Jack Smith's art is so precious that it cannot be exported. You know: seeming to be saying something complimentary when actually killing the chance of the economic possibility of my going to Europe. Everything on earth like that he's been doing. My life has been a nightmare because of that damn film. That sucked up ten years of my life. For a while I was being betrayed on an average of about twice a week to Uncle Fishook. It was like being boiled alive. People would turn me in because Uncle Fishook wanted to get me and everybody knew that . . .

(Sounds of the radio)

L: *Is that WBAI? Have you ever done anything for them?*

S: I tried; I tried. I went there a number of times. There are some dummies there. And I just had the bad luck of running into all the dummies, I guess. I get these incredible over-reactions because I'm a very strange looking person.

L: *What happened there?*

S: Once I was thrown out by the receptionist. I was asked not to wait inside the building. I was listening to their begging for money and it really gripped my heart. I went there. Four or five times. Every time I ran into some dummy at the place, so I just gave up. I wanted so much to help. It is the only source of information in the city. I think you have to be Jewish, number one. And normal, number two. The very first sign of the trouble *they had* was when they attacked the homo who had a program called *The Importance of Being Honest*, a gay program. And he was forbidden to put on one of his programs. People with their snot impacted voices that they paid for in college: their rumbling snot. They wanted normalcy. Later the whole station was turned off by the same management.

L: *In Italy, little independent radios like Radio-Alice have a more direct political impact on the population. It's starting in France too. They do it with very limited means.*

S: There's always been political art in Europe. There's never been any political art in this country.

L: *Do you consider your art political?*
S: I wouldn't put any program out now unless it had an overtly political title.

L: *How about your slide-show, do you consider that political?*
S: If you can put an explicit title on something implicit, that's almost enough – because you're giving the indication of how to see it. Not everything has to be cerebral at every moment. . . . But the title does have to be explicit. The title is 50 percent of the work. That's why I shudder with the title of your magazine. You have that chance to say something.

L: *A title is language, and I'm not sure language can be that effective.*
S: But thoughts can. The world is starving for thoughts. I worry about the thoughts. A new thought must come out in new language.

L: *So it didn't really matter if you actually had a slide show or not because you've advertised the title: the title is sufficient.*
S: Almost. You don't have to see the slide show as far as I'm concerned. The slide is entertainment, the icing. I mean there's a thought, there's a socialist thought in it, but the information and all the intellectual content is being conveyed by the title. You can become so explicit that you can state something the world didn't know and needs to know and this you can state very clearly in the title. The images could be made to mean anything, but the title's got to be explicit because it's your only chance. You have to struggle to make more of it more and more explicit, but, still glamorous. If it is not done glamorously, it's no good because it wouldn't have been dramatized.

L: *What title would you choose now for* Flaming Creatures *if you had a choice?*
S: Let me think, a new title . . . I have to think about it. . . . What's its

content . . . there never was any content. "Connecting Sugar with Hollywood," maybe . . .

L: *You mean your film was some sort of parody of Hollywood?*
S: It has a lot to do with it, yes. It took place in a haunted movie studio. That's why those people were coming and going like that.

L: *Was Hollywood really on your mind when you made the film?*
S: Of course. My mind was filled with it. . . . Everybody is filled with Hollywood.

L: *Did you watch television?*
S: Not until later. Then I became addicted to it. . . . No longer though.

L: *What sort of thing did you read?*
S: My favorite book was *The Count of Montecristo*. Sinclair Lewis is my favorite writer. They think they're through with Sinclair Lewis. I just finished a book of his called *King's Blood Royal*, in which the most typical WASP in the world finds out that he has one percent Negro blood; and then the book ends with everybody in the neighborhood marching on his house with rifles. But it could be about any minority group.

L: *What do you think of the gay movement?*
S: They've become a ghetto, already: they just want to talk about gay things. They're trying to cut it off from being in any context.

L: *Don't you think it's becoming something of an industry too?*
S: Oh sure, of course. It's just one of the unexpected bad side developments of it that's making it possible to be so happily ghetto-ized. But that's where the people in the theater are supposed to be coming in and helping the atmosphere. And, you see, they're not. I took my program to a gay theater, and he couldn't understand how it was gay, because he was unable to see it in a context. If it wasn't discussing exactly how many inches was my first lollipop, well then it wouldn't be anything they'd be interested in. And so I couldn't get this gay theater. It was one

of the places I tried. Getting theaters is one of the 7 labours of Uranus.

L: *What was that: "I Was a Mekas Collaborator!"*
S: I put the ad in the paper and then I didn't go to the theater. The ad was as far as I could get with a lobotomized, zombified . . .

L: *What do you mean by that?*
S: That if a program has any intellectual interest at all then it can only be given one or two nights – but you can be entertained to death in this country.

L: *Is that the slide show you want to present?*
S: That slide show is just the same mass of slides: I've been showing it for years. Every once in a while I have a new shooting session and add a new scene to it. Nobody has ever complained. It's always, you know, completely interesting. The Penguin Epic is all new, though . . .

L: *Why did you put that Swastika there?*
S: Nazism and capitalism have melted together by this time. I think that Nazism is the end product of capitalism. That's why I don't bother with words, because to me it's only a matter of if a thing is given to you or taken from you. And the words are only going to be twisted around someway by somebody somehow. For instance, you can make the word *socialism* mean anything on earth.

L: *That's why Burroughs uses cut-ups: to try to prevent the words from being twisted around.*
S: Oh, that's one way.

L: *It's an extreme way.*
S: That's the wrong extreme. What I mean is the extreme in the other direction – by being more and more specific about what you're thinking. The title is supposed to serve the idea. If I am lucky enough to get a socialistic idea . . .

L: *What do you mean by a socialistic idea?*

S: To me, socialism is to try to find social ways of sharing. That's all. And to replace the dependence upon authority with the principle of sharing. Because it's very likely that there would be much more for everybody, thousands and more times for everybody if things were shared. We're living like dogs from all the competing.

L: *Were you ever competitive? Did you ever believe in that?*

S: Yes, of course, when you're young, it's drilled into you, and you have to slowly find your way out of it, because you find it doesn't work. Capitalism is terribly inefficient. The insane duplication, the insane waste, and the young only know what's put in front of them. . . . But then, by experience, things are happening to you and you find out that this doesn't work. I mean this is *not* productive.

L: *It produces waste.*

S: I looked through your magazine and I was repelled by the title. It's so dry, you just want to throw it in the wastebasket, which I did. Then I picked it out. . . . Listen: *Hatred of Capitalism* is a good name for that magazine. It's stunning, I'll never admit that I thought of it.

L: *I doubt that by saying something that directly you'll change anything. Language is corrupt.*

S: Listen, you are a creature, artistic I can tell, that somehow got hung up on the issue of language. Forget it. It's *thinking*. If you can think of a thought in a most pathetic language. . . . Look what I have to do in order to think of thoughts. I have to forget language. All I can do with no education, nothing, no advice, no common sense in my life, an insane mother I mean, no background, nothing, nothing, and I have to make art, but I know that under these conditions the one thing I had to find out was if I could think of a thought that has never been thought of before, then it could be in language that was never read before. If you can think of something, the language will fall into place in the most fantastic way, but the thought is what's going to do it. The language is shit, I mean it's only there to support a thought. Look at Susan Sontag, that's a phenomenon that will never occur, only in every hundred years. Anybody like that. She says things that you would never have thought of. And the language is automatically unique. Whatever new thoughts you can think of that the world needs will be automatically clothed in the most radiant language imaginable.

L: *Have you ever thought of another type of society . . .*
S: I can think of billions of ways for the world to be completely different. I wish they would invent a scalpbrush. Do you realize that there is nothing on earth that you can brush your scalp with? . . . I can think of other types of societies. . . . Like in the middle of the city should be a repository of objects that people don't want anymore, which they would take to this giant junkyard. That would form an organization, a way that the city would be organized . . . the city organized around that. I think this center of unused objects and unwanted objects would become a center of intellectual activity. Things would grow up around it.

L: *You mean some sort of center of exchange?*
S: Yes, there could be exchange, that would start to develop. You take anything that you don't want and don't want to throw out and just take it to this giant place, and just leaving it and looking for something that you need . . .

L: *And there wouldn't be any money?*
S: Then things would form the way they always do around that.

L: *Will people still own anything?*
S: Yeah, I don't mind. . . . Buying and selling is the most natural human institution: there's nothing wrong with that. . . . Buying and selling is the most interesting thing in the world. It should be aesthetic and everything else. But capitalism is a perversion of this. Nothing is more wonderful than a marketplace. It gives people something to do . . . and it can be creative. Wonderful things come from commerce . . . but not from capitalism . . .

L: *What do you mean exactly by landlordism?*

S: Fear ritual of lucky landlord paradise. That's what supports the government.

L: *You mean property?*

S: The whole fantasy of how money is squeezed out of real estate. It supports the government; it supports everything. And it isn't even rational. When is a building ever paid for? The person that built the building is dead long since, and yet it can never be paid for, it has to be paid for all over again, every month. That's as irrational as buying a pair of shoes and paying for them again. It supports the whole system that we have to struggle against. We have to spend the rest of our time struggling against the uses they make of our money against us.

L: *They call it "rent control." That's exactly what it is about: control through rent.*

S: But if the whole population has no conception of how irrational that is, that's how far they are from doing anything about it, or any of the other things that oppress them. All the money that runs the government comes from the fantasy of paying rent.

L: *As if we owned something.*

S: Alright. So we don't own it. But do they own it? People that live in a place and maintain it and build it, why do they own it less than the government? Then you're saying that the government owns it more than you do. And that's also silly.

L: *The difference is that in a capitalist country you owe money to an individual and in a communist country you owe money to a state. It still holds . . .*

S: Well, you don't own your own property . . . but even if you could understand that, why would you understand that, why would you understand that somebody else has some claim, or owns, your property.

L: *You mean then that everyone should own what they use?*

S: You want to start making more laws and more rules. But that's how a lot of strange things began . . . from the expectation that you need all the laws and rules . . .

L: *But if no one had to own anything . . . if you use something, you don't have to pay for it, but it doesn't belong to you.*

S: What's so incredible about that? There is a new movement called Housing in the Public Domain – maybe the first idea on the subject since feudal times. I never had sunlight. I was always so naive I just kept taking places that had no sunlight. But the next time I move there will be some sunlight involved, somehow, coming through a window, or anything. But I can't build it; I can't be permitted to build my own house. You can build exotic architecture or strange houses if it's outside the city if there are not other people around that would complain. All the complaining!

L: *You want to build an exotic house?*

S: I'd like to invent a building that wouldn't be a rectangle, that would utilize the pouring qualities of cement.

L: *It would be closed?*

S: I don't know what in the world it would be. It would be open in the middle: sunlight could come in the middle. They cling to rectangles because it's the preferred shape of capitalism; it's easy to manufacture a rectangle, to manufacture the components of a rectangle. But why should I live in a house for the convenience of the manufacturers? I think the normal idea of the house is more circular, whatever it is, and it would have an opening for sunlight to come in. The house would be arranged in that way. It would also have all the ugly non-design of manufacturers banished from it. Everything to do with water would be in one place and it would be in the form of a waterfall; and it would be enclosed, and plants would be happy there; washing the dishes would become a polynesian thing, it would not be an ugly thing washing the dishes; and washing clothes, taking a bath would also be done in this place; the dishes would wash themselves. It would use much less water; all the water would be utilized; there wouldn't be any wasted water; the waterfall would be turned on and off, of course. It would be in the central part where the sunlight is . . . the water would be mixed with the sunlight, a steamroom would then be created, steam is very healthful, it cleans your lungs. And I can imagine anything on earth like this. But if I try to build it there would be a million laws saying that I can't build it.

L: *It sounds like a building you could build in Miami.*
S: I heard of someone building their own building in Miami, and the city officials made him tear it apart ten times until he got every little thing just to comply with the city regulations. So you wouldn't do it in the city. You might do it outside the city. As long as there aren't people complaining. And then this would dispense with the ugly rectangular monstrosity of the kitchen sink; bathtubs wouldn't exist. All this duplication wouldn't exist; it would save space. It's got to be built to be a model to do away with the ugly designs that now surround us completely.

L: *I think it is like art; as soon as there is a model it's going to be duplicated and then it becomes an industry. It's very difficult to avoid that.*
S: That's what I want: I would want them to duplicate my ideas. But all that's happened to me so far is that my idea that I never had doesn't register – and they duplicate my icing. I know how just a thing like the ugly design of kitchen sinks destroyed my childhood . . . 'cause I had to fight with my sister all the time over who had to do the dishes. It was the ugliness, the ugliness of capitalism, making it impossible for anybody to live a life that isn't made ugly.

L: *Where did you grow up?*
S: In the midwest. My father's family were hillbillies in West Virginia. They went to the hills because they wanted to be more independent in the first place, and then they became more independent because they were living in the hills. Hillbillies, nomads, gypsies are natural anarchists.

L: *Do you like that?*
S: Yes, basically I'm an anarchist, that's not to say that I think there will

ever be any state of anarchy, but I don't think that you should stamp out anarchy. . . . You need it to flavor other ideas, because anarchy is the giving part of politics. In this country they have stamped it out, and made it a dirty word, made it synonymous with chaos. . . . They want to tell you that it's the same as chaos. It isn't. All it means is without a ruler. And if people don't try to make a start of getting along without authorities, they will never be in a position where they are not being worked over by these authorities. And so naturally they don't like anarchy. We have never had anarchy, but we do have chaos. There's always going to be the government agents that are going to be throwing bombs, saying that the anarchists did it, to set up a reaction.

L: *There are so many rulers now. Authority is everywhere.*
S: They're dreaming of more authority.

L: *I could do with a little more chaos myself.*
S: All it is is an idea of gradually working toward doing things without authorities. Under an anarchist system you would phase authorities out slowly, as much as could be. That seems a fantasy, just because it's been so stamped out and ridiculed. Until the twenties you could go anywhere in the world without a passport. But they want to put you in the frame of mind where you accept more and more authority. You just are required to go through this ritual in which you give them the right to tell you where I can go. And if you don't, you'll be clapped in prison.

L: *It is not easy to live in the way you want and not suffer from it.*
S: I don't mind a certain amount of trouble. I can't take these exaggerated doses of pasty cheerfulness of capitalism in which you have to be happy all the time. That can only produce a crust like Warhol. I don't want to be too happy. I don't want extremes, I mean getting pinnacles of happiness. I can't live with it. What goes up must come down. I tried it. I was a pasty celebrity, I was very fashionable ten years ago . . . is this being recorded?

L: *Yes.*
S: (laughing) Wonderful. I was hoping it was. I was very fashionable but

I couldn't live with it. I will never, never go near anything like that again. This was the golden gift of Uncle Fishook to me. Please let him keep the blessings of publicity. I must say that before that happened to me, I actually believed like everybody else that I could not continue to exist unless I got a glare of publicity. You see, attention is a basic human need. It's terribly important. If the baby doesn't get attention, it won't be fed.

L: *If society makes you unhappy, then it has won no matter what.*
S: I don't think so. I can be happy from being unhappy, if I know what I'm doing. I mean I have to struggle against Uncle Fishook, that's my job, and I'm not running away from it. Everybody else that has been worked over by Uncle Fishook has just faded out, folded up and creeped out of the city. But I won't do that. Usually in life nothing is ever clear cut. How many people are lucky enough to have an archetypal villain for an adversary.

L: *You can find Uncle Fishook everywhere.*
S: When an Uncle Fishook falls into your life you have to fight it till the end. It's been dropped into your life, it's not the most glamorous problem, but it's been given to you to struggle against. . . . This is something for me to do something real for me to address myself to. You're telling me I should forget it in order to be happy. I don't like it, but what's the alternative?

L: *Do you know Nietzsche at all?*
S: It's probably trash because he was jealous of Wagner. I don't like his attitude towards Wagner. It was just the typical, very mediocre attitude expressed in very fancy language, but it was the very typical *Village Voice* attitude toward anybody that is making a success, but a success based upon their need to transform somebody into an object, and then sacrificing him.

L: *Nietzsche defines a nihilist phase which corresponds to what you call "anarchist": to question everything. There is a second phase which is more interesting: once you've realized what everything is and how it works, how* *it's going to repeat itself, endlessly, you just step out of it, and affirm other, positive values. You don't waste any more energy criticizing and destroying.*

S: Tell me what I am to do with the energy. I'm supposed to rush into the turquoise paradise of the Bahamas? After two days, I would be bored. I've got to have something to hate.

L: Flaming Creatures *was about fun, not denouncing.*

S: I made a comedy. Now I want to make a drama. The movie I'm now preparing is going to be an Arabian Nights architecture film and it will be in Super-8. 35 millimeter is insanely wasteful. And it's never cleaned. It gives me the horrors. Uncle Fishook represents the idea of expectations from authority, which is also perfect for me since I could spend the rest of my life demolishing very happily. I can be happy in this way. You couldn't, but it has just been my lot to have to clean out the toilets. I mean that's the job that's been inherited by me in life and I have run away from it. I spent the last fifteen years running away from it. Nobody wants to open a can of worms, but that's the thing that has been handed for me to do. And maybe that's a part of all bigtime manufacturers and capitalists, that they're Uncle Fishook. Maybe I've found a key to them in some way from having to deal with the evil that's come into my life.

Semiotext(e) 3, no. 2 (1978)

This redaction attempts to recast what seems, on tape, a characteristic rant on the topic of Jonas Mekas and the saga of Smith's career. It does contain revelatory digressions on the powers of thought, but rote Smith commentary on property ownership, capitalism, and architecture. The tape suggests the interviewer's interest in what Smith might have to say about William Burroughs, but Smith, occupied with his own thoughts, offers little in response. Smith signs off on the interview as though he were its author, and provided its title. Lotringer recalls that Smith was reluctant to accept another title that emerged from the conversation: "Hatred of Capitalism." Together, they produced the illustrated layout aboard a subway. Scott MacDonald writes in his introduction to *A Critical Cinema* (University of California Press, 1988): ". . . filmmakers whose work is of considerable interest to me were capably interviewed just at the time when I felt ready to talk to them: Sylvère Lotringer interviewed Jack Smith for *Semiotext(e)* in 1978, for example." Pity. (E.L.)

PENGUIN PANIC IN THE RENTED DESERT

SINBAD GLICK: These are the slides, when I first met Yolanda. I was a starving young actor in Rome and uh . . . I was hired to be the attendant that took the penguin out for its morning visit to the Colosseum and bring it back. And another attendant took it to church later in the day and . . . but this was before she started making movies, and uh . . . but even at this time she was . . . the world's most notorious penguin. It is the morning after the night P.P. Entwhistle, the head of Sunnyset Pentagram Motion Picture Studio . . . opens the cigar box Yolanda la Pinguina was kept in between films to renew her contract, and found her very *very* dead.

(to SECRETARY) The box has been here two days. Where will you take it after . . . when . . . later this afternoon when you . . . uh . . . leave work?

GLICK: It's uh . . . This was a . . . an early Yolanda Pinguina slide show. This one was called "Exotic Landlordism in the World." Another secret of acting is in your uh . . . most dramatic moments you contrive to be peeling onions.

SEC: Does that go along with this list of acting that you just gave me?

GLICK: Yes. Those are other rules of acting.

SEC: Jack's Rules of Acting.

GLICK: No. Not mine.

SEC: No? Basic Rules of Acting?

GLICK: It's a proclamation put out by P.P. Entwhistle, head of the studio.

SEC: One.

GLICK: The same P.P. Entwhistle whose . . .

SEC: Don't . . . don't mention it, please. Can I read this first?

GLICK: Yes.

SEC: 'kay.

One. Do not indicate. Do what must be done as it would exactly be done. Exaggeration is not necessary.

Two. Repress gushes of emotions so that it comes out slowly and naturally as in your sweat. This keeps the audience in suspense and makes them work so they have to try and figure out what is happening.

Three. Remember staging. For example. When having a nervous break-down, a crucial climactic element: look for the hot point on the stage which may not be the most obvious, Front Center which should be reserved for narrators only. But look for a more subtle but extremely hot area where all emotions can be seen.

Four. Remember aspiration is not a cause for an N.B. [1] Failure is. Remember aspiration is not a cause for an N.B . . . Failure is. The scene after P.P. Enstwhistle's call is one of desperation because I have lost my last chance at becoming a star. I have failed on the ladder to success as a starlet.

Five. Express my state of mind, primarily despair, in this production, through my relationship with the objects on the stage, remembering not to stick to the solitariness of my desk. Gestures of the most minutest details tell elaborate stories.

Six. Be aware of the other characters and objects at all times. Concentration is of the utmost importance.

Seven. Although reality should not be stuck to without exception, it is essential to remember the logical coherent steps that go into everyday living. Do not skip around or do things haphazardly, just because you are on stage. Things must be believable.

Eight. Do not go directly to the center of your trauma. This is unhuman. Beat around the bush a little bit. Remember, gestures and details tell elaborate stories.

GLICK: Uh . . . I was just thinking. I think I need three dance numbers in the production instead of two.

SEC: And how . . . but what about everybody else?

GLICK: Let them eat cake.

SEC: What about my dance numbers?

GLICK: Well . . .

SEC: Just because I'm a secretary I don't get any dance numbers?

GLICK: No. But I think that . . . two would be very nice.

SEC: What, two for me?

GLICK: Yes. It would contrast nicely with the three . . .

SEC: With the three or four or five that you might take? Just because you own all the chiffon doesn't mean you can dance around like crazy you know. And those are my mittens. They were given to me for my birthday by a very good friend of mine.

GLICK: What happened?

SEC: Well you keep making me cut the onions, I mean, slice the oranges... they're all soggy.

GLICK: Well no, I mean . . .

SEC: Do you suspect foul play?

GLICK: What? Yolanda had no enemies. Except . . .

SEC: Well what about Joanne La Barracuda, I mean, they weren't exactly friends. It's a tricky business.

GLICK: Joanne Barracuda films have dropped off at the box office in the last few years. And she . . .

SEC: She's a vicious, vicious woman. She can't be trusted. I thought the studio should have dropped her long ago . . . but I mean what good is my opinion, I'm just a lowly secretary, but . . . *vicious* woman. Beyond belief. I mean such pettiness. I could not *believe*! I mean Yolanda was just a sweet . . . she wasn't cut out for this business.
You have to have a heart of stone to get anywhere.

GLICK: It's very unexotic. . . . Where's the bottle. . . . Keep some of it there, I mean make a balance between them, you know. . . . You don't think that Joanne Barracuda dreamt of stepping into Yolanda's wedgies...

SEC: Oh definitely!

GLICK: And stealing . . . and stealing the very forehead earring of exoticism off the forehead of Yolanda la Pinguina?

SEC: You know that is the dream of every starlet on this set. I mean if you haven't noticed . . . I mean the star has been ripped off her dressing room door countless times. I mean I just started painting it on . . .

GLICK: Well. Next day on your dressing room they glued a star, or pasted a star.
I never knew which. What's . . . (sings "There's No Business Like Show Business") Next day on your dressing room they . . . glued a star. Is that it?

SEC: On your dressing room they glued . . . pasted . . . glued . . .

GLICK: Stuck a star . . .

SEC: Stuck. Stuck. Gum.

GLICK: Pinned a star . . .

SEC: No. Pinned. Not that. Stuck. I guess it's sort of, you know, I mean . . . use your own imagination. I think it's stuck.

GLICK: Placed a star. Or put.

SEC: Placed. Like a heavenly entity.

GLICK: Why don't you take the box out to . . . out to . . . the Penguin Pits.

SEC: The dreaded Penguin Pits?

GLICK: Yes. The Sacred Penguin Sacrifice Pits.

SEC: But the ghosts. It's . . . haunted. I don't know . . . who could do it . . . I think it's really bad luck to take her to uh the Penguin Pits without a proper . . . fune . . .

GLICK: Permit?

SEC: Yeah.

GLICK: Yes. Possibly yes.

SEC: And also the Sacred Penguin Rites haven't been performed yet . . .

GLICK: The what?

SEC: Sacred Penguin Rites? Haven't you heard of them? The ones that were written on the sides of the pyramids? Sacred Penguin Rites? I think that it would be incredibly bad luck for her to be placed out there . . .

GLICK: Placed out where?

SEC: In the Perilous Penguin Pits.

GLICK: Without what?

SEC: Without the Penguin Rites.

GLICK: The Penguin Rites?

SEC: The Sacred Penguin Rites.

GLICK: Well, that's the . . . you mean the Penguin Sacrifices, you mean? Of Lucky Landlord Lagoon. Of course. (music swells, long pause) I love drinking orange juice. It's so much like drinking . . . lobster blood. The orange juice squeezer is a strangely Bagdadian thing. It uh . . . it is shaped like . . . like an Aladdin's lamp. But . . . it's round. Uh . . . and it comes to a Bagdadian point! Also the orange juice itself is a very Bagdadian thing.

SEC: Mr. Glick, do you think that Bagdad is the answer to Hollywood?

GLICK: Well . . . I . . . I don't know, I wouldn't want to give you a pasty answer.

SEC: I'm just looking for help for the answer to . . . stardom.

GLICK: Maybe you could talk P.P. into becoming, letting you become the replacement for uh . . . Yolanda . . . the creature that his latest proclamation uh according to which he's looking for . . . someone has to be found to be Maidenform de la Pinguina anyway.

SEC: I don't have a chance. He just uses me as a receptacle. To fulfill his every whim . . . I mean he knows the trashy things he makes me resort to. He promised stardom long ago.

GLICK: Take the onions . . . and the next time he has an erection . . . and uh . . . peel onions, I mean, and uh . . .

SEC: Excuse me Mr. Glick I'm in a bad way. I . . . It's like I've reached this obstacle and it's impossible to surmount. I mean . . . an impasse impossible to surmount. An impasse impossible to surmount.

GLICK: Why . . . did you figure out who you were?

SEC: Uh . . . I'm not sure what her name is but there's this secretary in this movie, I think it was, I mean definitely it's an element of Kathe . . . and then it's a cross between the secretary in this movie but I don't know the name of the movie, actually . . . I'm working on it. I'm working on it. Why, can you tell?

GLICK: It must be very nice for you to have the day off because he surely wouldn't . . . wouldn't call the day after the death of the penguin.

SEC: I would hope not. I mean this man has no decency? I mean this is a very sad day in Hollywood. . . . What a woman. What a penguin. I doubt anyone could fill her . . . feathers. 'Cause she was . . . her diamond encrusted tailfeathers.

GLICK: Uh . . . It's very sad not to have . . . the penguin in the cigar box, isn't it. You should leave this, you know and . . . uh. . . . And . . . uh . . . and uh . . . and just uh . . . (music swells, long pause:) You could . . . uh . . . I think . . . I think your hair has come out of the bun.

SEC: My hair?

GLICK: I think the hair has slipped out of the bun. What kind do you use . . . what . . .

SEC: Sticky buns from South Station . . . was it the souvlaki stand – no it was the kielbasa stand . . . all night kielbasa stand. The best coffee in town!

GLICK: That looks like a bagel. Is that a bagel?

SEC: It's a honey bun. A sticky bun.

GLICK: It looks like the crocodile might have got at it though.

SEC: These glasses hurt my eyes after a while. It's a little warm in here. So do you really think that I have a chance at becoming Maidenform de la Pinguina?

GLICK: I don't know. But let's . . . let's take the box . . . out to the uh . . . excavation . . . and uh . . . and . . .

SEC: Just a second. Let me get dressed. . . . Shall we take the box?

GLICK: Hum?

SEC: Shall we take the box?

GLICK: Yes. In case P.P. Entwhistle calls, uh . . .

SEC: Tell him I'm putting my galoshes on.

GLICK: Yes. Tell . . . tell him . . . that . . . tell him that . . . What is your character's name?

SEC: Um. It's uh . . . uh . . . Peggy the Secretary. No?

GLICK: Tell him that uh . . . Miss La Rue . . . and uh . . . Mr. Glick were attacked by one of the crocodiles but they'll be back in the office . . . uh . . . later this afternoon.

VOICE: Later this afternoon.

GLICK: Yes. We're just going out by the uh . . . out by the uh . . .

VOICE: Lucky Landlord . . .

GLICK: . . . out by the big clumps of hibiscuses uh . . . but we'll be right back. We might be cutting across the Desert of Exoticism. . . . But we should be right back in a little . . . get a breath of fresh air . . .

VOICE: I'll tell P.P.

GLICK: That we were attacked by one of the crocodiles but it's nothing . . . just a few . . . uh . . . [2]

TAPE ENDS

Penguin Panic in the Rented Desert was presented September 23-26, 1981, at the Eleventh Hour Gallery, a living-loft cum underground performance space near Boston's South Station. The event was described in some detail in the February 1982 issue of the Boston Film/Video Foundation journal *Visions* by Kathe Izzo (who lived in the Eleventh Hour and plays the secretary Miss LaRue). Izzo's account, "Do What Must Be Done as It Would Actually Be Done," suggests that the tape transcribed was the third or fourth performance.

1. nervous breakdown.

2. In a conversation on the reverse side of the tape cassette, Smith offered Kathe Izzo the following postperformance critique:

You have to be like one of the writers if you're acting in a thing, and if it's this kind of theater you have to take responsibility for being one of the writers of the thing. . . . You see, all this mass of material can be communicated but only through handling the props, only by doing a million things . . . because that's how you tell. If somebody were crumbling apart with emotion you wouldn't know it unless they happened to be peeling a carrot at the time. . . . Something like this . . . this is what acting is. I mean you have this mass of material in your mind. All right. Dramatize it! Convince us. It doesn't *sound* like anything I ever heard of in human nature, but if you're convinced that this is what's motivating your character that is in line with human nature, then convince me! Dramatize it! Convince me and convince the audience! . . . Yelling the thing or telling somebody and dramatizing it is not necessarily the same thing . . . look for the carrot! Find the carrot to peel that will crumble in your hands as you are overcome by emotions! This is all any acting school tells you. You have to at least know that. That there is such a thing. I'm sorry if its bad news. Or if it's a personal insult. . . . But this is how people with widely differing ideas can have some common language on stage. To get *out* the ideas. And it's the same, it's the rules of everyday life. I'm telling you that if the carrot didn't crumble out of the hands of the person, you wouldn't know. Otherwise it would just look like a person standing there thinking. Put the carrot in their hand and let it crumble when they're having a nervous breakdown, and you'll see, and this is what the stage is. And it's a lot of other things too. But you have to know some of these things.

appetizing makeups.

IN ~~[crossed out]~~ A BUNGALOW IN HOLLYWOOD

IT IS ~~[crossed out] ~~IN HOLLYWOOD~~....

THE MORNING AFTER ~~[crossed out]~~
THE NIGHT P.P. ENTWHISTLE,
THE HEAD OF SUNNYSET-PENT-
AGRAM ~~[crossed out]~~
~~STU~~ MOTION PICTURE, ~~[crossed out]~~ OPENING
THE CIGAR BOX YOLANDA LA PIN-
GUINA WAS KEPT IN BETWEEN
FILMS ~~[crossed out]~~ ~~HER~~ TO RENEW HER
CONTRACT.......FOUND HER ~~DEAD~~....VERY-
VERY-
DEAD....!
~~(NEEDS ECHO)~~

WHAT'S UNDERGROUND ABOUT MARSHMALLOWS?

I have to live in squalor, (chewing noises) all day long playing hide and seek with odors. I want to be uncommercial film personified. That's the . . . oh wait . . . have to live in squalor all day long playing hide and seek with odors . . . no kidding folks. They love dead queers here. (music) Still, it is very nice to be let out of the safe every ten years whenever there's some retrospective program. We underground film makers are kept in the safe at night. We sleep in the safe standing up. It's like a – uh – French foreign legion of interior decorators. Everybody there for some reason – some because they've betrayed their fellow film makers . . . actually I don't like to be fucked. Others because this is their only chance and they know it. Others to seek the certification of Uncle Artcrust. (music swells) Kindly old Uncle Oldie, I remember how I first became involved with Uncle Roachcrust. It was in the early '60s and I was Donald Flamingo, living at home, minding my own business. My business card read: "Everything from Ancient Egypt to 1940s" . . . but I was getting old, or at least my muscles were contracting and my hair was turning white. And I had a sort of a grayish color, and uh, I started naturally to think of retiring to an Aloha community. Which I did. And one evening in the dining room, as I looked around the plastic palm trees with the uh, mothers pushing the baby carriages among the plastic palm trees . . . it uh, it seemed to me that the orchids were whispering about *me*. It seemed that they were saying "He is the next to be sacrificed!" (sound of Portuguese *fado*) Uh, and uh, the olive sun was blazing in the cream cheese sky. The gravy oozed down the side of the volcano of mashed potatoes. I felt the carbonated tide of Coca-Cola rising in my veins closing off my pores. (chewing noises) I woke up on the floor besides an empty box of Chips Ahoy. Later I found myself swaying to and fro in front of the window of a confectionary shop. (sound of tango) Then I was hanging around the uh, the uh, Artcrust Archives. And uh, one day a kindly old man appeared on the steps, and uh, offered me a job as a sugar zombie. And uh, which I uh, accepted. And uh, every day the uh, I and the other sugar zombies would be marched out of the safe into the underground sugar beet pits.

No, no, the underground sugar beet, no, no, the underground desert of sugar beets? . . . of uh, and we had to toil in the oozing marshmallow paste all day long to harvest these enormous spoiling uh, sugar beets like giant enpurpled Andy Warhol noses . . . like huge bloated machine-gun turnips that out of the enlarged pores of which would ooze a sugar syrup . . . and uh. . . . they putrified immediately if you touched them. It was loathsome . . . loathsome . . . the foul and purple things . . . it was hellish. Well, anyway . . . (coughs)

Long pause with exotic music and tango

Uh . . . This is an intermission. Let's take a ten minute break, could we please? I was even in the middle of the story, but I'll remember where . . . I hope you don't mind . . . because there's already been you know enough good stuff already to compare with even the new – the latest hit – *Penguins of Penzance* – (music)

Break in tape

. . . the door to the safe was open a bit . . . and uh, so I uh, I crept out and uh, passed out into the corridor. The light hurt my eyes very much I remember. Then presently my eyes became used to this, and I noticed a small pointed doorway that was the uh, doorway to the uh, to Uncle Filmcrust's Hollywood Underground Sugar Hell . . . (music with jungle noises) Uh, and so uh, I went through this doorway and down some circular stone stairs, and at one end of a giant cavernous vault, I uh, I saw among the giant boiling uh, uh . . . what are those things . . . what? Giant uh, (sighs) – I wish this roach would leave this stage! Please, go away! Shoosh – MEOW – meow, kitty, kitty . . . giant vats of uh, boiling sugar paste and among these I saw Uncle Artcrust bending over a film duplicating machine. And I realized that this was the reason or the means by which his operation could be understood, and he was duplicating the film left in the safe overnight by anyone he could succeed in having the characteristic two evening engagement of . . . of . . . of uh, the uh, Lucky uh, Landlord Underground, uh, Desert of Blue Glitter.

(pause) Because of these hellish experiences, you see, sometimes my mind wanders . . . uh . . . let's see, where was I? . . . "Desert of Blue Glitter" . . . uh . . . and then I realized that he was sucking the travel out of all the baby film makers! (mock Chinese music) . . . and the thought occurred to me of dashing at him and knocking him away from the machine, and then . . . I hesitated for a few moments and then unfortunately one of my rings fell on the floor – cheap jewelry is always crumbling off of me . . . and, and horrified I saw that Uncle Pawnshop had spun around . . . I hardly had time to pick up the ring, when he had gathered up the pile of film cans and darted out of the room through another pointed doorway, and slammed the door and uh, turned the lock. So uh, I thought I may as well go back into the safe . . . and because he had (whisper) escaped again, and . . . so I may as well go back into the safe because that wasn't the worst of it anyway . . . the worst part of all was that no one . . . (fumbles through pages) . . . oh, uh, Uncle Archives darts out of the pointed doorway and locks the door. And I realize that uncle Pawnshop has escaped again, and uh, I may as well go back into the safe . . . but the worst of all is that nobody thinks I'm acting . . . or that I'm not a great an actor . . . or even an actor . . . at all. Or that this stuff isn't even acting. (pause with Latin music)

If you couldn't move in your theater seats . . . if you couldn't tear your eyes off of the actor, then it must be good acting . . . (long pause with piano music)

Ooh, how can I get some coffee? How can I get some coffee? Does any-body have some coffee left over? Someone must go for me for coffee . . . oh, thank you. There's nothing in here . . . it's empty! I need an exotic volunteer of the Desert of Cheerfulness . . . come on. It has to be a black with one sugar . . . (gong pause) You see, you should have gone, because you saw this scene last night . . . (music with jungle cries) Uh, one of the secrets of great acting is that always to contrive to be chopping onions . . . in uh, some uh, dramatic moment, and uh . . . so I think I'll uh, start the onion soup now . . . (sound of peeling) The uh, uh . . . uh . . . uh, Phyllis Newman is dropping in for onion soup . . .

SIDE TWO

(music)

. . . 1941 (gong): The Invisible Woman. 1941 (gong): Boss of Bouillon city. 1941: That night in Rio. 1941: Raiders of the Desert. 1941: Moonlight in Hawaii. 1941: . . . South of Tahiti. 1941: . . . Bombay Clipper . . .

Break in tape [1]

(gong) Siren of Atlantis. 1949 (gong): Hans le Marin. 1949: Portrait d'un Assassin. 1949: Il Ladro di Venezia. (gong) 1950: . . . Amore e Sangre (gong). 1951 (gong): La Vendetta del Corsaro. 1951 (gong) . . . (music)

Break in tape

(music) . . . the first thing you notice as you enter the round socialistic movie studio . . . the temple of the sacred brassiere of Maria Montez . . . is the open central courtyard where the public may arrive in the morning with their lunch to uh . . . to pay to watch movies being filmed in the sunlight. . . . They may spend the entire day, and in the projection follows for one low admission price they take their seats in circling balconies and as the lights (mock Italian music), . . . sunlight travels around the court-yard . . . the actors, decor crew and audience change their arrangement to follow it. . . . This is respect for the sun – also not uh, negation of nature that is the basis of capitalistic so-called theater. In this theater the first consideration in every decision is good ecology before art and before everything. The uh . . . because uh . . . (mumbles) The center of the courtyard is the work area. The sets are around the inner wall of the courtyard and are built permanently and are also architectural experi-ments to serve for various purposes – they are not destroyed after the production is finished . . . but changed as needed by being adapted and added to, and uh, also serving the practical needs of the audience. For example, the multi-level Arab cafe set may continue to serve coffee and mineral water even in the background of the filming or . . . in this way, or if it would produce a tweeky effect . . . (pause . . . music ends)

Uh, oh mother of God, without my glasses, already. . . . Let's see . . . (shuffles papers . . . pause)

(cocktail music) Oh, more volume perhaps a bit, maybe . . . let's see. (sighs, shuffles papers) Uh . . . Toward the round movie studio itself, all the, everyone acts in the spirit of cleanliness . . . a clean movie studio is a happy movie studio . . . (bell) . . . If I may say so: personally, I do not know how to make art on a dirty floor . . . (music ends, shuffles papers)

The bar is open. (music) Salami and formaggio and whole grain bread are sold for sandwiches in the gateway of Basra and tomatoes, strawberries, and onions are growing for sale on the backs of the Nile set. In a section of the balcony are the actors' dressing rooms . . . they are open to the courtyard so that with binoculars the audience may see the actors applying their make-up . . . the shooting schedule is in the order of what hour the sunlight is where, and the audience watches with fascination the struggle of the set decorators, the set dressers to adapt the permanent sections around the inside to the particular needs of the story being filmed. (music) When the last ray of sunlight has disappeared the audience retires to the Rattan Room to get drunk! This takes a couple of hours. They also have the choice of retiring to the Deewan Pensione to get high . . . this can only improve the enjoyment of the events that will follow. . . . (movie music swells) The great gong sounds and this is the signal that the projection apparatus is in readiness in the courtyard under the stars . . . (pause) the uh, the unedited rushes of the previous day's filming just back from the lab, are screened. Immediately after that the uh, all the previous semi-edited footage of the previous production is . . . shot thus far, is screened. Then there is an intermission, wherein the audience has the chance to improve their heads, compare notes, copy phone numbers (rustle of papers) . . . make sentimental arrangements for the evening, relieve themselves, and wheel and deal . . . and otherwise wheel and deal. . . . The hanging brass lamps dim out . . . (asks the audience to turn on any light – anybody, anywhere) . . . somebody cut that light on the word "screen" . . . and that's the cue for the projector. . . . The hanging brass lamps dim out, and the completed previous production at the studio – They Demolish Opera Houses Don't They? – flashes onto the screen . . . .(sound of furniture moving) The music petered out at that last moment? I needed it to cover that last . . . (furniture noises, hooting noises)

. . . Those onions . . . uugghhh . . . phew . . . . .(tango music)

TAPE ENDS

Smith first presented *What's Underground About Marshmallows?* on October 9 and 10, 1981, as part of a series of underground films at the Theatre for the New City. This performance, tape-recorded October 10, 1981, provided the text for Ron Vawter's *Roy Cohn/Jack Smith*. During performance, Vawter discreetly listened to Smith's tape, using it to prompt his timing and inflection. (E.L.)

A xeroxed flier from late 1981 announces that *What's Underground About Marshmallows?* will have its premiere on November 21 at the OP Screen and be performed thereafter once a month, every third Saturday night. A second sheet offers a schedule through March 20 as well as the following precis:

> Is the underground exotic? No, this is how we got
> Hollywood. Unreal film-babies unable to do business,
> losing money, slave class of lovable landlord class
> who irrationally operate theatres in the style of the
> passive executive, as just more of the old sacrifice-
> betrayal context, the continuing betrayal of the
> socialistic impulse.

You know the kind . . . where we go from co-op, to
distributor to cinemathque to archives . . .
imperceptibly dissolving from one to the next
incarnation. . . . So he'll never have to go hungry again
like back in Europe.

Welcome through the pointed doorway to the
underground night of Uncle Archives Lucky Landlord
Underground Vaults of Filmcrust!

1. Coincidentally or not, the tape breaks at the point where Smith would intone Montez's best
known movies – *The Mystery of Marie Roget* (1942), *Arabian Nights* (1942), *White Savage*
(1943), *Ali Baba and the Forty Thieves* (1944), *Follow the Boys* (1944), *Cobra Woman* (1944),
Gypsy Wildcat (1944), *Bowery to Broadway* (1944), *Sudan* (1945), *Tangier* (1946), *The Exile*
(1947), *Pirates of Monterey* (1947) – and picks up again with her last Hollywood vehicle.
(J.H.)

What's underground about Marshmallows?

A tour through the underground night of Uncle Archives vaults of filmcrust. Guided by Jack Smith. Once a month performance & film series.

GRANT APPLICATION (September 14, 1982)

Regarding the grants I have received
and am applying for:

Dear Persons,

In 1978 I received $10,000.00 from the National Endowment for the Arts
for my project SINBAD IN THE RENTED WORLD. As I show in the budget,
the money has been spent on costumes, interior sets, props, and my own
time. I have also received $500.00 from the Creative Artists Public
Service Program in 1981. Finally, this year I applied to the New York
State Council for the Arts for $10,000.00.

I am requesting that my project be considered for funding again. After
FLAMING CREATURES (1963) my next film EXOTIC LANDLORDISM OF THE
WORLD took twenty years to finish. And now I realize that finishing a
film for me is not a matter of years but decades. The film sample, which I
am prepared to deliver personally for reasons described in the enclosed
sheet, from EXOTIC LANDLORDISM (referred to as NORMAL FANTASY in my
enclosed bio.) will give some idea of the work involved in totally editing
a color film. Films we see today are at best only twenty percent edited.
The art of the silent film was killed by sound. The dialogue tells the
story, not the editing. No commercial studio would attempt to one-hun-
dred percent edit any color film because they would have no way of
knowing when or if it would ever end. This sample is what a totally edited two and one-half hour episodic color film is supposed to look like.
Now I am nearing the end of pre-producion for an Arabian Nights film,
another impossible project.

Everything in an Arabian Nights movie has to be made by hand. It
requires a more appalling amount of money and work than I would have
ever thought possible. I would have given it twenty years anyway
because I am better organized but now I am almost frightened by the
work I see ahead. That is why, even though I received a $10,000.00

grant in 1978, I am applying for an additional grant for the same project, SINBAD IN THE RENTED WORLD. [1]

I am preparing photographs of the project's sets and costumes to give you an idea of the detail involved and the progress made.

Very truely

Jack Smith

Smith continued to seek support and venues for his work during the 1980s. Drafts of letters in his own hand suggest that Smith is the primary author of them, and not a collaborator in their gestation, as in P. Adams Sitney's disclosure of involvement in the writing of Smith's 1964 Ford Foundation proposal. These letters vivify his attitude. (E.L.)

1. The following plot synopsis is included in an untitled flier.

The ruined house of Bagdad remembers its story: Sinbad's birthday celebration, his recital of the voyage he made before his more well-known voyages, when he was still Sinbad the dancing boy. He recalls for his guest's amusement the last night of the "Oily Moment Cafe" where he danced and the incident with the wallet. Unable to go back to the "Oily Moment," Sinbad becomes drawn into the spell of the crooked "Your Big Moment" radio program that comes from glamorous Roach Crust Island. He sails to be in the radio audience. The ship is torn apart in a storm of commercials and the wreckage flung on the shore of a false Lighthouse, a part of the complex of buildings that includes the Pawnshop and the Brassiere Museum from whence is broadcast the "Your Big Moment" radio program. Sinbad awakens upon the shore, thinking vaguely that he might have been Sinbad the Tailor, but isn't sure. . . . He must dive for pearls, finds and keeps a forehead-earring-shaped-pearl, and is cheated out of it by Uncle Pawnshop. Later, after buying a tailor business and sitting up late every night for ten years to make the peacock costume, he investigates the Pawnshop. A crab woman buys the pearl and takes it to the Brassiere Museum where he follows her and is given free moral advice to work at the Sex Museum to pay for screen tests to be in the "Your Big Moment" radio program finale. Working in the darkened Sex Museum, Sinbad is drawn into a mistaken identity confusion with Hamlet by a voice from a coffin. He steals a dollar from the giant Crab Ogress' purse to go to a Maria Montez film, and the Ogress rushes at him with a fly swatter. Sinbad escapes on the dollar bill, the Ogress swatting in a frenzy of roach murder. The screen tests return – the "Blue

Fishnet" number is especially good, and Sinbad appears in the "Your Big Moment" radio program, only to learn how the priestly caste poisons your relationship to something basic with a mixture of promises, lies and hatred. In the confusion of the climatic roach stampede, the Lobster in his final priestly disguise with the forehead-earring of exoticism in his back pocket, is drowned in Plaster Lagoon and now is hardened over.

They say—O it's
so easy for him
we will make
it hard for
him. They don't
know how to
respond to
it because
They have
lost their
underst-
anding
of any work.
They
think
its
their
due
that
its not
a gift
and was
paid for
by the
artist
as they
can
tear
it away
from me.

JACK SMITH FILM ENTERPRISES, INC.

Heiner Ross
Metropolis Cinema
Hamburg, Germany
July 1987

Dear Mr. Ross,

I am intrigued that you would consider stepping out of the ordinary to the extent of presenting a program of mine to your audience.

Since "Flaming Creatures," I've been involved in a working method that might be called "LIVE FILM." Some of the work goes on through the screening itself. Someday, this might be imitated for there is almost no other way to dislodge film out of the bankrupt state it is now in which can only be goosed up by more and more violence and synchronized chatter.

With a program of mine, you get: (A) Extra trouble: I am experimenting with various records as the film is projected and making other small corrections. This could be turned to advantage as a glamorous selling point. Often, there is repeat business because people can see the film gaining power as corrections are made and that is a new kind of film excitement and (B) full houses.

I'd want your best terms and your best extended run. Yes, I'd travel with this and cooperate in every way to make substantial profits for both of us. In the U.S. payments for films are determined by a split of the house. Is that the system you use? What are the net and gross figures?

I am not as familiar with *Metropolis* as I suppose everyone has assumed. I never attended a program there although I'd have gone to the restoration of the Russian silent film, but I left Hamburg just before it opened. If I could be sent a schedule, I could take it to someone who could interpret it, and design a program suited a little better to the character of the theatre, but, in general, I'm always expected to show "Flaming Creatures" in Europe so I'd bring it. (45 min. / BxW / Synch. sound). I'm sure too about "Exotic Landlordism of the World." (BxW / 45 min. / Records) and the rest of the program would be filled in from a huge mass of color film that will someday be two full length films. (Records)

I appreciate the politeness of your response since you can never have seen a properly mounted film program of mine. In my later work, I have taken as my point of departure that moment before the arrival of sound. (The art of silent film was never perfected and that is what I have spent the last 20 years in doing.) The story is rendered pictorially and, drawing upon psychology, something like the logic of dreams is deployed, rather than the rigidly anecdotal chronology which is all that is know in film at present.

Also unlike current film the images are based on the techniques of European, pre 20th Century Story-telling Art which gives the films a gorgeously Baroque look and a grandiosity and elegance that is definitely considered undemocratic in the U.S. but which I suspect may have the potential for a major success in Europe.

My films are not conceptual or art-school cutie-pie; they can have the broadest appeal (as Art did before the silver-spray democracy of the schools.) An idea of them may be obtained by imagining a huge Veronese beginning to breathe and palpitate with a hallucinatorily slow movement.

If we could agree on a series of perhaps 3 or 4 trips to Germany, which would be ever better, all the implications of this could be realized fully and to our mutual benefit.

Yours sincerely,
[Jack Smith]

STATEMENTS, "RAVINGS", AND EPIGRAMS

What practical meaning does original have, applied to the imagination. We originate nothing. The origin of all things is outside ourselves. We have only to scratch the icing to find beneath – centuries of icing.

O Goddess of cinema – I have come to your altar – my arms full of props – Mother Cinema, Jealous Mistress I have yielded to the special demands of the cinema affected Rapture All the secret delights of Stardom – Artificial Ecstasy – The Orchid Rot that wastes the flypaper landscapes studded with the bones of dead Hippopotami on the comeback trail.

Normalcy is the evil side of homosexuality.

I am queer but don't ask me to live in the shadow of the cunt of your girl friend.

When you have police everything looks queer.

A normal is me who knows what a faggot is.

If it weren't for fairies, what would normals have to think about? They learn early somehow that the fairy is the sacrifice.

My darling I find myself thinking about you when there is nothing on my mind.

And doesn't capitalism make human relationships except for sex all but impossible?

God must want to be shocked.

Your glamorous friend.

I only seem fantastic because I am so practical.

The title is 50% of the work.

In my last program I was a Yvonne De Carlo for the Lucky Landlord Underground. But I lied.

Why are people horrified that I have human characteristics?

I have Art for Rent – I am my own agent, I'm not some fantasy object you can talk to about money or who doesn't have to make a living. It is perfectly alright to talk to me about money just because I'm an artiste.

Brochure: "I can be rented"

Xavier Cugat – the Surgeon General of Latin Dance Music.

Do we need consumer crabs to remind us to eat?

I know I've done a lot of bagdadist things in my life

If I still have any friends it's because they aren't thru with me yet.

Isn't Christianity the worship of betrayal?

Theatre? There is no such thing as teachers there is only the apprentice system – and Maria Montez knows I can use a couple of helpers right about now. – Jack Smith [phone number]

Whom the courts would destroy they 1st make angry.

Pick the envelope – not the stamp.

It is not the insult which is insulting – it is the intention to insult which causes the insult, and which is indeed the insult.

Glamorize your messes.

I can be funny when I'm alone.

Art is all day long – when anyone wants to adjust anything they are using art.

Sadism always begins with flattery.

Fashion is an ugly business.

Socialistic Art uses glamour – it was paid for by Maria Montez.

The critics are the hand maidens of the Lobster.

I overcame pastiness.

The search for the world's most exotic dentist.

Any moment America will arrive at scientific reasons for aesthetics.

Question – How can I be sure I don't need an exotic consultant?

I'm in a position of the golden baby fantasy – idiot who did the work, made the great plays, etc. And nothing happened. They want it to die after two rehearsals.

The dull but honest Flaming Creatures.

Experimental film is when the end of the film is stuck to reel in dirty scotch tape and when you start to re-wind you don't put your finger on the tape to make sure it doesn't separate from the reel.

If there was anything good about Rome it was their baths, not their courts.

I'm afraid to give anybody anything. It seems to instantly destroy their personalities. I have to find a way to give that doesn't look like giving. I don't want to be destroyed . . . and yet I do want to give.

I am one of the very few artists not trying to peddle academic art. In other words I put everything into a program. It leaves me weak and burnt out for weeks afterwards. It becomes almost a physical ordeal besides being an ordeal of academic politeness.

Bring dead film back to life thru doorway to Bagdad.

Art History if you will notice is nothing but the history of brainpicking.

The horror of rectilinear lagoon – they react to you so they can rob you!!

Clapitalism is when you must kill in order to earn a living.

I am really an extremely material person – I'm the only normal man in Bagdad.

Picked apart by brainpicker services – they won't approach you with a deal but will approach you as a trick objectified.

What doesn't exist is important.

Fashion – it makes up for an awful lot.

To be or not to be Normal.

I am always put in an exotic mood by a glamorous cocktail.

I may look a little pale, but that's because they don't let me out of the safe very often – deliver rent checks . . .

Lets take Maria Montez for granted.

Kill time – see a movie.

I just want to plunge into the color blue.

Thanks for explaining me.

The orchids don't look too good this year.

Easier for Y de Carlo to pass through eyelette.

Would you hold it against me if I couldn't stand for this?

These notes appear in journals and letters, on file cards, the backs of envelopes, as marginalia in books and elsewhere. Smith referred to the posture of some of these as "ravings." Among them are a few he used recurrently, as apostrophes or mantras, sometimes citing them in abbreviated form. (E.L.)

SOUNDTRACK OF *BLONDE COBRA*

Ginger Rogers sings: "Let's call the whole thing off."

Jack: Yes, we are drowning, drowning in a sea of nescience, completely soaked in an ocean of nescience, yes. And the whole world is nescient too.

We will now start all over again.

Katherine McGinely's crushed, blood drenched oh body and face showed horrible violence of her death.

Boopoo be doo. Da da deda dum, bo oh de oh do. Poo poo pe doo. Oh yes, a mother's wisdom. Gloria Swanson wore size two shoes. Gloria Swanson had a pair of shoes for every dress. Bo do de oh, a mother's wisdom, (hysterical laughter). Gloria Swanson had a million pairs of shoes.

WNYC radio announcer: Twelve noon by the century old chimes in historic city hall. This is New York, the city of opportunity, where nearly eight million people live in peace and harmony and enjoy the benefits of democracy.

Jack: Yes, nescience, ya nesience is the thing it's true; yes, nescience brought me to you.

This corpse is obviously dead, I can see that because it's lying there so waxen and wan. To be dead, to be truly dead, is a wonderful blessing, oh Renfield my friend. Ravish, ravish, ravish, dum de de dum ravish, ravish, ravish, ravish, ravish, ravish, necrophiliac uhh huh huh huh now I'm ravishing the corpse, ravish, ravish, ravish, ravish, ravish, uuuuh necrophiliac longings, necrophiliac fulfillment!

Leprosy is eating a whole in me, my teeth are falling out, my hair has turned to sauerkraut. La da de da dam la la de da de de la la le lum la la la lam la dum de dum. Heh heh heh.

There was once a little boy, a little tweensy, microscopic little boy and he lived in an enormous house and there were ten rooms. And it was such a large house or so it seemed to the little tweensy boy, I mean, it had so huge and overwhelmingly cavernously enormous . . . it had ten rooms!

All right. Mother Mother M o t h e r M o t h e r Mother Mother Mother Mmmmmm dade de da de de da dum. And then the little boy would just scamper back to the room that he had come from and look for his Mother, but she was never there, and so he would finally pass out and just fall onto the floor and fall asleep just weary with loneliness and longing and frustration and frustrated longings, until, until when the shadows were lengthening and the sun was drooping he would hear the front door open and, and he would rush out and dart out into the hall-way and there, and there was his Mother . . . and she always had little white bags from the ten-cent store and they always had certain kind of chocolates in them, the brown, the droplet kind, the chocolates that had little indentations on them and they came to peaks on top! And the little ones had the white stuff all over them and, ah, and he would eat it and she would give him some but not much, just a little because she would save most of it for herself and ah so ah well ah and then, she'd go away again. Next day, same thing all over again. Mother Mother Mother Mother M o t h e r M o t h e r and then, and there was a little boy that lived upstairs you see it was a two family apartment and ah and – a two family house! and then one day the little boy found the other little boy that lived upstairs the family who lived upstairs in the upstairs floor and the little boy who was less than seven, the lonely little boy, the lonely little boy was less than seven, I know that because we didn't leave Columbus until I was seven, I know it, I was under seven and I took a match and I lit it and I pulled out the other little boy's penis and burnt his penis with a match!

Oh God . . . Oh Creator I mean uh . . . how can. . . wait . . . never mind! Never mind!

Riverview, Riverview, Riverview Nursing Home, Riverview, Riverview, Riverview Nursing Home, Riverview, Riverview, Riverview Nursing Home – Riverview Nursing Home.

La Reve De La Purité. La Reve De La Purité de Madame Nescience . . . wait . . . how do you say nescience in French? La reve de la purité de Madame Nescience, Ma*dame* Nescience. Dream of purity. Madame Nescience lies on her couch. Ah. She is dreaming. She is dreaming of old musty memories, memories that she thought that she had forgot or so she thought but you see they came up in a funky mass of ah exuding effluviums from the musty past that . . . covered with moss, and funk. Anyway, Madame Nescience is sitting as a nun . . . uh . . . she, Madame Nescience wanted when she was a little girl ah a little girl she wanted to be a nun! and uh in her dream anyway, the dream goes on and on but in part – She's sitting there, and she's the Mother Superior, she's become the Mother Superior of a convent – I don't know if this makes sense to you – uh but one of the Sisters comes in, Sister Dexterity. "Madame Nescience, oh oh I mean I mean Mother Superior oh I've just come from the girls, from the girl's dormitory. Madame Nescience. . . . I mean Mother Superior, oh I've just come from the girls, from the girl's dormitory. Madame Nescience . . . I mean Mother Superior! You see this is a dream! Mother Superior, there's an eruption of lesbianism in the girl's dormitory. "Oh oh" . . . "What is that you're saying Sister Dexterity? That's a lie, that's a damn lie. I won't have such lies going around in this convent. Turn around, turn around, I say; turn around and drop your habit and bend over. Now hand me my rosary. I'm going to give you nineteen lashes with the rosary! hahahahahahahahahahahahahaha!" "Oh Madame Nescience. . . . Oh I feel so pure! Ohohohohohohoh I think I'll go out and throw myself on the altar and give my body to God! ahahahahahahahahahah!"

What a turgid dream, what a turgid dream indeed. Madame Nescience proceeds down millions and millions of winding stairs to the girls' dormitory, to the Sister's dormitory ahahahah, and there she find ah well ahha the girls, ah the young ladies have thrown themselves upon a plaster of ah well Jesus. I mean ah they've been shoving the thing up their cunts and uh they've been reaming each other with their crosses. The scene is a mad disorder of broken rosaries and torn and tattered habits and cunts. Oh God. O what a scene, and Madame Nescience comes in and uh says, stately, in a stately way of course, "Girls, I want all of you to bend over and all of you to drop your habits. Now I'm going to go down the line and paddle you . . . with the cross. Hmmmmm, the silver cross. Alright Girls, bend over! Hmmmmmah hahahahahahahahahahaha ha ahahahaha-hahahahahaahahahah hunhuhnnnnnnnhnhnhhunhy! Now, all of you girls sit down and say a million Hail Marys and uhm uhm a thousand uhm Our Fathers and uhm, an octillion, octillion . . . oh let's see, what shall it be – ? *Jack sings EVIL WORKS to early '30s German tango:* God is not dead. God is not dead, he is just marvelously sick. Evil works, evil works, evil works against itself, but it can't harm you because you're not evil: you will remain unharmed, yes you will remain unharmed. God is dead. "God is dead and man is abandoned," Jean Paul Sartre! God is famous! and evil is practical. Oh yes. Evil is practical hahahahahahahahaha! Evil really works. Evil really works, yes, evil works and not against itself, against you! The results of evil are forty thousand dollars a year on dividends alone; imagine what the capital must be! If money is the root of all evil, give me the whole tree! Dadad ahahahahahahah. Evil works, evil really works! aaaaaaah. God is famous but evil is practical dadadededdam, god is not dead, he is just marvelously sick, dadadadedadem ahahahahahaha-haha-hahahahahahaha!

Madame Nescience tells Renfield My Friend's fortune: Ahm ahhhhhhaham Well, I've gone into a trance, and I've had a convulsion and I ah ahm I stared into the thing there, you see. I scrutinized the palm of your hand there – well ah I think you'd be better off dead!

Nescience!!!

Miss Montez was admirable, she refused to wear brassieres for one thing, she . . . well ah; Riverview, Riverview . . . Nursing home.

Astaire, Rogers from "Swingtime" track: "It would look kind of funny if we denied the marriage now. "I don't know what to do." "I don't either." "The word is eether."

Jack: "Why shave . . . when I can't even think of a reason for living?" Jack Smith, 1958. Sixth Street.

Astaire: "Alright, the word is eether, no use squabbling about it. That will get neither of us nowhere."

Rogers: "The word is neether."

Jack: "Life is a sad business," Greta Garbo, Yes. O truly spoken O Greta. Yes.

Astaire: "You say eether and I say either, you say neether and I say neither; eether either, neether neether, let's call the whole thing off."

Jack: "Life swarms with innocent monsters," Charles Baudelaire. (Scene in the Kitchen of Iniquity). Oooooooooh! Sex is a pain in the ass. Sex IS a pain in the ass.

Baby Music

Jack: Bo do dee oh. Oh de do doo, poo pee doo. A mother's wisdom . . . ahhhh! A Mother's wisdom has dragged me down to this! A crummy loft! A life of futility! Hunger! Despair! Bo be do do, boo pee doo ahha. What went wrong? What went wrong? WHAT WENT WRONG?!

Film Culture #29 (Summer, 1963)

As published in *Film Culture*, the transcript of *Blonde Cobra* is not absolutely complete. Among other things, it omits the brief conversation between Jerry Sims and Bob Fleischner that opens the film and concerns the Gershwin song "Wintergreen for President" from the musical *Of Thee I Sing!* (J.H.)

The Great *Blonde Cobra* Collaboration: In early 1959, during one of the many periods when Jack and I weren't speaking to each other, Bob Fleischner picked up on the filming of Jack Smith and Jerry Sims where I had left off after shooting *Star Spangled to Death* and *Little Stars of Happiness*, etc. The cinematography was done almost entirely in Jack's place with some scenes in Jerry's apartment, both on the Lower East Side. From what I was told, Jack set the scenes in his place and Bob would come over on the weekend and film. They were shooting two separate films at the same time, but there was a falling out between them after shooting about 10 silent 100' b/w 16mm. rolls and one 100' color. As with my shooting (Bob had sometimes assisted) there were no retakes, no intended cutaways, no shooting script.

Bob told me that Jack hadn't been able to pay Con Ed and was living by candlelight. His cat knocked over a candle and there was a fire in which Bob's remaining raw stock, stored with Jack, was damaged. Bob demanded blood from a stone, that is, reimbursement before he'd continue, while Jack insisted that the fire was "an act of God." Impasse. Bob told me that Jack spent much time admiring his image on a table editor, but neither Jack nor Bob figured they had anything but two hopelessly aborted projects.

Bob then took his camera reversal originals back from Jack and shelved them for some months before showing them to me. Having no idea of their original story concepts, not missing what wasn't there, I immediately declared that there was a film imbedded in these rolls of disparate shots. Bob gave over the material to me winter of 1959 to do with as I wished, never inquiring about the progress of the work, nor seeing it – nor did Jack – until there was a complete editing of the film less sound (and visual accommodations to sound) spring of 1960.

But the completion of the film was entirely upon me economically as well and I was chronically broke. Summer 1961 I showed the film at the Sun Gallery in Provincetown with *Little Stabs at Happiness*, both accompanied by 78 rpm records. In the spring, *Little Stabs* first went public at an open screening at the Charles Theater on the Lower East Side. Jonas Mekas was in the audience. He somehow tracked down my name and address and I got a postcard from him asking me to phone him. I did, from a public phone, and he said he wanted to program the film. I was elated but had to tell him it was the camera original, I had no prints and couldn't afford to make one. He told me to take it to a lab and bill it to him (as proxy for Jerome Hill). I sagged, but then told him there was another short film, *Blonde Cobra*, also very close to completion, also in need of its accompanying soundtrack. He told me to take that film to the lab too.

I borrowed a phonograph and a reel-to-reel tape recorder from Rene Rivera (later of Mario Montez fame), and Jack and I struck a truce (after the final rupture of our working friendship – end of summer 1961) and he came down to my Brooklyn Bridge loft for two recording sessions. I had prepared some lines I wanted him to speak for specific placement against the visuals, statements he had made ("sex is a pain in the ass") during our six years of self-educating fooling around or in his style ("this corpse is obviously dead, he's lying there so waxen and wan"); and of course the *Dracula* line, "To be dead, to be truly dead, is an o wonderful blessing, Renfield my friend," that Jack and Jerry repeated to each other countless times daily. But there were also lines that Jack improvised to the mike and all the songs were improvised, again with no second takes. I would play the beginning of one of my dozen or so old 78s until Jack would nod signifying that he was ready, the record would start again and he'd rip. He supplied the Arabic music that's played early in the film when he's loving himself in the mirror. I improvised on the harp of a dismantled piano while he recounted the story of Madame Nescience ("I mean Mother Superior!") with no prior discussion or rehearsal.

I selected sections for transfer to optical sound and cut the optical track to the images. It took forever and then was shown on the same program with *Flaming Creatures*, midnight at the Bleeker Street Cinema, April 1963.

The only thing Jack said to me after a prior screening at my loft was, "You made it heavy." He told a mutual friend the film embarrassed him. Bob seemed mildly gratified as I recall, but I may be exaggerating his enthusiasm. Jerry Sims demanded to know when he could expect money for his acting. Jonas was appreciative; after his first viewing of it in the N.Y. Filmmakers' Co-op office (unbelievably, Stan Brakhage arrived in New York at the office during that screening and stood for a while looking at the 18-foot-high projected image with his expression signifying that here was the epitome of New York sickness) Jonas quietly said, "I didn't expect it to be tragic." He told me to bring the picture and sound originals to the Co-op for safe storage, where they were to rest on a sofa for a few days before their intended shipment to a vault. During this period many people went in and out of the Co-op, and one of them I've always assumed was a Jack Smith pal, lifted the cut track. (Years later, Jack would sic a lawyer on me to prevent screenings of the film.) Only one print was in existence and I now had the prospect of composing the track again from the original tapes. It was absolute hell, dyslexia left and right, and took almost another year, even with only the soundprint to guide me and with only the most minor changes.

KEN JACOBS, FEBRUARY 9, 1996

Who knows

O David –

Every time I get high something untoward or highly human or improper or heart tugging or in bad taste or . . . you took it very well. O it left me with a bad sinus attack – been laid up for most of the week. Feeling wretched. Feeling disjointed. Have been thinking of nutty product names & I can't seem to stop – like: Cutex fire escape remover and new foaming chunky style eye refreshing paste with fur balls etc. & I drove Joel off the razor's edge when I got home that morning. She fled to the Bronx & left me with no help for the movie so I got Sheila & instead of finishing the movie according to the script I shot some pure psychotic footage of Sheila SINGING . . . singing mind you – I was reeling I was so zonked that morning behind that c. . . . Now I spend my days wondering where to insert that footage of Sheila singing. . . . Life is so funny. If you only knew. . . . Staying with Tony now. Peter Pan existence – when I'm 40 I'll be playing in a sandbox. Androgynous, unconventional, sportif, fascinating creature . . . sometimes momish (momeish?) & waspish but always in the mood for Tropicana orange juice in wax coated golden brazen upturned hindoo containers. No use tonight – better to go to bed.

Write soon o

Love

Jack

Written to David Gurin in the early autumn of 1962, soon after the completion of *The Beautiful Book* and during the last stage of the *Flaming Creatures* shoot, this letter was read by Gurin at the Jack Smith memorial at P.S. 122, October 16, 1989. In introducing the letter, Gurin recalled Smith's distinctive language: When [Jack] was faced with some particular platitude that he liked despite its platitudinousness, he would say, "Moldy, but true." Or when he came upon something he really like a lot, and this I'll never forget, he said, "O veracity-drenched!" (J.H.)

ACTAVISTIC, ACTION PACKED, ACTION ACTING OF PFA
HAMLET and the 1001 Psychological Jingoleanisms of Prehistoric Landlordism of Rima-Puu

"We do have revolutionary ideas about acting and we are testing them on the world's most abused play, " says Jack Smith, director of the Reptilian Theatre's production of *Hamlet and the 1001 Psychological Jingoleanisms of Prehistoric Landlordism of Rima-Puu* now playing at the SoHo Theatre, 131 Prince Street, through September, and the director of the film classics *Flaming Creatures, Normal Love*, and *No President*. The staging of this play is influenced by movie techniques and by discoveries made by Smith at the Plaster Foundation of Atlantis, an experimental free theatre that has produced, over the past few years, among other plays, *Claptailism of Palmola Economic Spectacle*, and *Spiritual Oasis of Lucky Landlord Paradise*.

The *Reptilian Acting Technique* has been known for years to other artists – Ronald Catchscene, Stagedoor Starsnatch, Umgawa Pilferplot, and Beggarstaff del Procenium. A certain other theatrical director has made a reputation in Europe and America off a minor invention at the Plaster Foundation, glitter makeup. Like tomatoes it was thought to be dangerous, until recently; it was only in the 20th Century that tomatoes began to be eaten. Certain other things were invented at the Plaster Foundation of Atlantis, especially the realization that thinking is interesting on stage. "It was there I realized," says Jack Smith, "if an actor just stands on stage and thinks, the audience knows what he's thinking and it is more direct and clear than memorized lines. Ultimately, memorized speech is possibly the least dramatic thing that can happen on the stage or anywhere."

In the Reptilian Acting Style there is no taking responsibility for anything you can not believe – the play should be tested in this way by the actor – not be submitted to by him. The R.A.T. is an extension of the common sense approach of Lee Strasberg, it would seem to be saying let's *not* pretend – this could affect thinking.

Rodney Werewolf, who stars as Hamlet in this production, has been trained in the Reptilian acting method which was developed at the Plaster Foundation where he appeared in *Boiled Lobster Easter Pageant*. Appalachia Allen (Gertrude) has been seen in *Dark Tomorrow* on television and her most noted film was *Cropdusters' Revenge*. Douglas Desmond (Claudius The Ghost) was the hit of *Cocktails Before Noon* and in recent years he has appeared in the Mrs. Paul's Fishsticks commercials. Kitchenette del Casino (Polonius) has been doing things around the P.F. since his first appearance as the Brassiere Boy of the Sewer in *10 Million B.C.* He also played in The Theatre of Lascivious Intrusion in Philadelphia, Annenberg School of the Arts. Florence Luck (Ophelia) played the madonna in *Claptailism of Palmola Economic Spectacle* at the P.F., and she also appeared in *Sinbad and the Seven Labours of Uranus*.

The Reptilian Acting technique rests on the premise that everybody already is a fine actor, that everybody in fact uses drama every moment of their lives, and that it's the fault of the theatre that nothing of this can survive on the stage because of the way that the drama is stamped out of everything on the stage, which has turned the actor into a Jelly – a thing that can only memorize lines; in drama school, the director has been stamped out of actors, the designer has been stamped out of them and everything else. It's resulted in the seemingly dumbest members of society becoming its actors.

"Actors have to pretend they are not directing themselves," said Rodney Werewolf over a freshly killed mouse at the Russian Tea Room, "and they have to use up their fantasy to keep the job so that by the time they hit the stage there is nothing left but what they've memorized. Reptilian acting farts on Naturalism," continued Mr. Werewolf, washing down his mouse with a Pepsi-Cola; "not only are students kept from memorizing, but they are encouraged to make a hash of it. Acting shouldn't deny glamour, Mr. Werewolf went on, "but instead treats it as an eternal human and humanizing thing. If more generals had Elizabethan costumes there wouldn't be time to be dropping bombs on other countries, as the

Reptilian staff has proved in its costume workshop, which has been making fashion news."

And the staff is Idi Hendricks (wardrobe mistress), Krash Kavanaugh (Hamlet's black costume), Kenje Kiratani (wedding cake), Isamu Kawai (Ox), The Daughters of Bilitis (tools), Johnnie Coffin, Carl Gallo (milking machine), Chris Kearns, Charles Leslie, Kazue Naito, Sylvia Carewe, Stella Waitzkin, Bill Holmes, John Diekman, Xerox Company, The Morrison Bakery (Mr. Danish), J.K. Quinn and Lois di Cosola (publicity), poster photo - ANI.

"We've been trying to avoid the spotlight," says actress Florence Luck, understudy for the production, "but we just finally have to face the spotlight, because we can't afford staying out of it." Since other directors wear out a discovery as soon as he discovers it, burning it down here and in Europe, Jack Smith says, "actually a discovery could be made every day by anybody, if the Western thing of having great plays to be memorized wasn't making mynah birds of us all. I know of someone who received thousands of dollars from a foundation to make a movie that's main claim to fame was it gave people epileptic fits. "They're supporting people to be junkies in a situation that parallels the Welfare thing of supporting only non-productive members of society. If I were to declare bankruptcy it would wipe out my rent dept – but would I be forced to move?" is the additive of another hard pressed thespian, who is several months behind in her rent. The Reptilian Theatrical Company has never been supported in such a way as the museums could leave the shrimp ends out and clean up on the pate de foi gras. Some will think *Hamlet* to be a pasty novelty. The play calls attention to Landlordism as the central social evil of our time. Instead of many social evils like the black problem, crime in the streets, welfare and dope, there is only one: it is landlordism which is magic, like paying sacrifices to the gods for protection to be left alone to do whatever it is you want to do.   **– Kitchenette del Casino**

Press Release/For Immediate Release: From the desk of: Dame Redd studio X 30 East 14th Street New York, N.Y. 10003

Received by Anthology Film Archives Sept. 10, 1971

SELECTED ANNOTATED BIBLIOGRAPHY
by Edward Leffingwell

PUBLISHED WRITINGS AND RELATED MATERIAL

Smith, Jack. "The Astrology of a Movie Scorpio." *Film Culture* 76 (June 1992): 23 – 24.

————. "Belated Appreciation of V.S." *Film Culture* 31 (Winter 1963 – 64): 4 – 5. Smith provides a sketch of this material in his journal, with additional information not included in the published version. He writes: "People who can't use their eyes complain about the bad weak trite ludicrous phony dialogue & story lines of Von Sternberg films. Von Sternberg got dos Passos to write the worst dialogue of 1936 for *Devil Is a Woman*. . . . He constructed ludicrous, exaggerated (*sic*) – Hollywood Nutty Spanish sets; made a wonderful mouldy – corny melodramatic atmosphere in which Deitrich (*sic*) could wax deleriously hammy. He turned melodrama upon itself and came up with a true personal fantasy. This was no Spain, even of the inept Hollywood imitation style, this was layer over layer of clutter, extras in rented costumes, light & shadow as it never existed in nature or even art up to this point, costumes that Deitrich must have had difficulty standing up in, in short a perfect artistic Spain that still could not stand up against ridicule since it had no defenses against ridicule. . . . How many critics must have waxed brilliant, missing the entire point of his works. He held that a film is something to look at. That the visuals tell the story. That the story can't be told twice. That the story that the words of the film tell can't be the same as the visuals (because forbidden themes can be expressed in images, but not in dialogue) that the visuals can therefore tell a richer story (being a visual medium) . . ." *Journal*: 29, 31.

————. "Capitalism of Lotusland." *Los Angeles: LAICA Journal* 19 (June-July 1978): 15 – 16.

————. "The Memoirs of Maria Montez or Wait For Me at the Bottom of the Pool." *Film Culture* 31 (Winter 1963 – 64): 3 – 4. In a 1985 introduction to a Random House edition containing his *Myra Breckinridge* (1968) and *Myron* (1974), Gore Vidal writes, "The silly-billies greeted *Myron* with predictable horror while my fellow inventors continue to use the book as a quarry." On the other hand, Myra/Myron playing havoc on the set of a doomed Maria Montez vehicle suggests Vidal's debt to Smith's classic reverie, down to, and especially including, the syntax. Both very much through the looking glass. In a journal entry, Smith begins to construct the "Memoirs" as "Maria Montez Flic. The Plaster Movie Studio broods in a deep shadow obscured by scaffolding . . ." *Journal*: 27.

————. "Normal Love." *The Floating Bear* 28 (Christmas 1963). Published by Diane di Prima and LeRoi Jones (Amiri Baraka).

————. "Notes for THE FORD FOUNDATION Application - Program in Humanities and the Arts." *Film Culture* 76 (June 1992): 24 – 25. Appearing with Smith's "The Astrology of a Movie Scorpio," this issue of the journal includes a handsome portrait of Smith by Melissa Meyer in Mike Sullivan's *No Smoking*, 1967, and a sequence of Wilhelm Hein photographs of Smith in a Moses narrative, a project by Babeth and Smith for Art '74, Kölner Kunstverein. In "Writing Jack Smith's Ford Foundation Application," published in *Film Culture* 78 (Summer 1994): 12 – 14, P. Adams Sitney explains that the application (denied) was written by Stiney, and not directly by Smith, based on their conversations, and at the instigation of Barbara Rubin and Jonas Mekas. Sitney was then nineteen and an "editor" (his qualification) of *Film Culture*. His conclusion – that the text was not intended to be published or survive – seems at least a moot point.

————. "The Perfect Filmic Appositeness of Maria Montez," *Film Culture* 27 (Winter 1962): 28 – 36 (illus. 33 – 36). This homage to Montez includes a series of stills and publicity shots from *Cobra Woman*, *Arabian Nights*, *Ali Baba and the Forty Thieves*, *White Savage*, and a truly wonderful photo opportunity shot of Montez with Eleanor Roosevelt.

_____"'Pink Flamingo' formulas in focus." *Village Voice*, July 19, 1973: 69. This dizzying diatribe praises John Waters' film for exceeding the reach of polite and suborned film criticicism, although it mainly consists of an attack on the criticism of Mekas and Andrew Sarris, both film writers for the *Voice* at the time. As free-wheeling and unpolished as the article seems, a surviving typescript indicates Smith's careful attention to turn of phrase. In that form, the title included the additional line: "Jobbing Critics Visit a Trailer Camp."

————. "Red Orchids" includes "Pfeffernus Flavored Aspirin," "Pasty Thighs," and "The Great Moldy Triumph." *Film Culture* 33 (Summer 1964): 19 – 23. A draft of the first paragraph of "Pasty Thighs" is recorded in *Journal:* 105, where Baroness Horsecock appears in another incarnation.

————. "Taboo of Jingola." *Village Voice*, Dec. 21, 1972: 75.

————. "The White Pig of the Medina." *The Great Society* (1967): 20 – 22. Ira Cohen and Richard Richkin, eds. Scrofulously horrific erotica, this reverie appears in developmental stages in Smith's early *Journal* as "Picture Book."

————. *Historical Treasures*. Edited by Ira Cohen. Madras & New York: Hanuman Books, 1990. In this compendium, a "Capitalism of Lotusland" variant appears under the title "Could Art Ever Be Useful?" *Rehearsal for the Destruction of Atlantis* appears as "Lobotomy in Lobsterland." Although the Hanuman version is a nearly word-for-word duplicate of the *Rehearsal* script, published in *Film Culture* in 1966, it does not identify the script as a "dream weapon ritual." The "ritual" itself is dedicated by Smith to Irving Rosenthal in the previously published version, and in other typescript versions. Variations in the Hanuman version include the use of "Mehboribeh" for the character who appears as "Mehboubeh" in *Film Culture*. The use of "Maria Montez" in Hanuman is in error: the reference is a stage direction for Mario Montez, who appeared in the 1965 production.

This section is followed by a piece identified as "Part Two," with Archives

Malanga as source. One typescript of the same work in the Jack Smith Archive of the Plaster Foundation is titled, in Smith's hand, "Lobotomy in Lobsterland," rather than "Part Two," "Lobotomy" apparently used in Hanuman to underscore the very real connection between the performance text and this extended essay. The Hanuman version transposes the first page of the text to an unlikely position near the end, indicating that the block of page one in the unpaginated typescript was inadvertently shifted to page four, so the Hanuman sequence in typescript source is 2, 3, 1, 5. The version printed in the present anthology demonstrates Smith's intended order. A close comparison of these two documents discloses very few other variations.

Elsewhere, what appears as "Remarks on Art & Theater" is cobbled together out of a number of different remarks made by Smith in the context of the give-and-take of "The Artist Versus the Hippopotamus," the True Comedy Planet symposium cited in this bibliography under "published transcriptions." Hanuman also includes "The Perfect Filmic Appositeness of Maria Montez," published previously by *Film Culture*. The volume is introduced by lines delivered by Cohen at Smith's memorial in 1989, at P.S. 122, and by J. Hoberman's *Village Voice* elegy on the occasion of Jack Smith's death.

PUBLISHED PHOTOGRAPHIC MATERIAL

Smith, Jack. *The Beautiful Book*. New York City: *the dead language press*, 1962. Published by poet and filmmaker Piero Heliczer, this handcrafted edition contains tipped-in black-and-white prints, small in scale, from Smith's extended photosessions of the late 1950s and early 1960s, including baroquely massed tableaux vivants. A drawing by Marian Zazeela is silkscreened on the cover. Participants in the photo sessions included Zazeela, Smith himself, Irving Rosenthal, Mario Montez, Arnold Rockwood, Joel Markman, Jerry Sims and Francis Francine.

————. "Brain Damage: Sorcery As Art." *Avant Garde*, 1968. Published by Ira Cohen and Bill Devore.

————————. "Buzzards Over Bagdad Underground Movie Flip Book." *Aspen* (December 1966). Andy Warhol and David Dalton, eds. The images sequenced here are billed as "from the forthcoming film *Buzzards over Bagdad*, a Cinemaroc North African Nicolodeon Presentation by Jack Smith." The thirty pages that follow the opening titles are introduced by a sequence of an oscillating fan in close-up. The camera pulls back to mid-shot revealing the fan resting on a small table covered with something like leopard skin. A female posing hand-on-hip becomes partially visible to the extreme right of the frame. As the fan turns, a second figure, in profile, wearing a "leopard-skin" turban and flowered, strapless shift, enters from the left. As the second figure passes the fan, the first figure is revealed to be wearing an elaborate hat. They gaze at each other, the left passing the right. The camera moves down, again including the fan and the first figure's hand on hip. The camera pulls into close-up and then extreme close-up of the flowered fabric, closer, the images more reductive except for the patterning of the fabric, closer, perhaps up, and concludes with a detail of dress and bare arm. The sequence is odd, deadpan, somehow suspenseful, weirdly funny, and recalls the opening sequences of the two figures and backdrop of vase and flowers at the beginning of *Flaming Creatures*.

————————. "Fear Ritual of Shark Museum," *Avalanche* (December 1974): 26 – 27. While Smith participated in Projekt '74, sponsored by the Kölner Kunstverein, he posed for a more or less preconceived "storyboard" sequence of images, many of them at the Cologne zoo. In *fumetti* – cartoon balloons of speech and thought issuing from the strip's protagonist – Smith appears as Ronald de Carlo, "who, in everyday life of Lucky Landlord Paradise, is a postman of Lotusland." He circulates rent checks from a monkey and to an eagle, while camels wander through several frames. Smith rehearses his complaints about the evils of landlordism, with an accusative aside concerning the Cologne museum, and finally, exhausted, lies down on the altar of property and waits ". . . until . . . The End."

The sequence was produced by *Avalanche* editors and publishers Willoughby Sharp and Liza Bear, with photographs by Gwenn Thomas, mechanics by Stephen Saban, copyright Jack Smith and *Avalanche*. Smith was associated at the time with the late German arts figure known as Lutze, who was attempting to represent Smith in Europe. She appears in some of the unpublished frames. In preparation, Smith developed a long-hand draft, and then a four-page typescript, which was again abbreviated and numbered in sequence, and further edited to fit the large scale, two-page format. Smith appears on the cover of the issue, which also featured Daniel Buren, Hans Haacke, Gordon Matta-Clark, and the Phil Glass Ensemble, among others. Thomas worked with the publishers on stories with other artists as well.

————. "The Moldy Hell of Men and Women, A Fotographic Essay." *Film Culture* 35 (Winter 1964 – 65): 33 – 39. In this photo essay, Smith sequences images related by their disparity. It includes a staged photograph of Jerry Sims with fedora, suit, aiming a smoking gun that was also published in a related sequence captioned "on the bowery" in *Scene* 8, no. 2 (April 1962). Both essays include couples in a park, the old, the young, and the cross-dressed. Smith used the title in a handwritten meditation on the pathetic horrors of the daily existence of the Munchkin family, whose aesthetic life "like that of zillions of other families was brutalized and crushed to nought by its own linoleum." The unpublished text includes this fragment: ". . . The mother darted to protect her greeting card album. She kneeled beside them and let her body slowly droop and her emerald green stole with gold metallic shredded plastic cascade down and cover the portfolio which also bulged with snap shots of powdered pasty babies in their coffins crushed together face to face in the portfolio . . ."

————. "Superstars of Cinemaroc." *Gnaoua* 1 (Spring 1964): 68 – 77. The images included in this photo essay derive from the sessions that culminated in the publication of *The Beautiful Book*. The sequence is introduced by numbered captions. The third proposes a future "flic" to be made in Rio de Janeiro, an event that in some respects did take place several years later, although without his stars. The central figure in the image related to this caption, a bare-chested Valentino hunk with pencil mustache, sideburns and white tights, is Rene Rivera, a/k/a Mario Montez.

—————. Stills from *Flaming Creatures* and *Normal Love*. *Film Culture* 32 (Spring 1964): 38 – 42. Several stills also appeared in a variety of publications, including several "men's" magazines.

PERFORMANCE AND FILM SCRIPTS

Smith, Jack. "Rehearsal for the Destruction of Atlantis," *Film Culture* 40 (Spring 1966): 13 – 14. This issue includes a photograph of Smith in Bill Vehr's *Brothel* and snapshots with Ron Rice.

—————. and Ken Jacobs. "Soundtrack of *Blonde Cobra*." *Film Culture* 29 (Summer 1963): 2 – 3

The Jack Smith Archive of the Plaster Foundation contains a number of scripts in various stages of development. They range from the (technically) published dialogue for Smith's *Secret of Rented Island*, an adaptation of Ibsen's *Ghosts*, to a shooting script for an unfinished film Smith essayed in Rio de Janeiro during carnival, 1966. Characteristically, they have any number of titles. As an example, the shooting script for the Rio footage is titled *Carnaval (sic) in Lobsterland*, but in a letter to an acquaintance in Brazil, Smith writes, "Naturally it's to America's interests to maintain confusion and cause and support the stupid revolutions. For this reason I'm tempted to call the film Snoflakes of Hotel Bagdad. But probably won't." He goes on to list other titles in another drawing: "A Night and a Day in Rio de Janeiro," or "A Balcony in Rio," "An Opalescent Afternoon in Rio." There are versions of an adapted *Hamlet,* an improbable scenario for *Sinbad and the Seven Labours of Uranus*, *I Was a Male Yvonne de Carlo for the Lucky Landlord Underground*, *White Pig of the Medina*, and others.

PUBLISHED INTERVIEWS AND TRANSCRIPTIONS

Brooks, David. "Free Association Interview with Jack Smith – April 23rd, 1964." *Film Culture* 77 (Fall 1992): 24-33. Young "montage" filmmaker David Brooks (*Nightspring Daystar*, *The Wind Is Driving Him Towards the Open Sea*), was appointed by Jonas Mekas to manage the Film-Makers'

Cooperative in 1962. Brooks lightly guides this segment of extended interviews as though it were a fictive documentary, revealing as much about his own technique as about Smith's construction of fable. Acknowledging the give and take of the interview format, the attempt at transcribing Smith's hesitation in phrasing his responses seems appropriate here rather than intrusive or condescending. Smith's improvised and extended, vaguely autobiographical narratives, barely interspersed with Brooks' occasional cues, are comparable in broadly referential information, syntax, and hyperbole to Smith's expression on the written page.

Lotringer, Sylvére. "Uncle Fishook and the Sacred Baby Poo Poo of Art." *Semiotext(e)* 3, no. 2 (1978): 192 – 203.

Malanga, Gerard. Interview with Jack Smith. *Film Culture* 45 (Summer 1968): 12 – 15. Malanga served as editor for this collector's item issue of the journal, sometimes referred to as the "Warhol Issue." Using what would become the signature, studiedly dumb Q & A technique that defined *Andy Warhol's Interview*, Malanga attempts to elicit Smith's commentary on superstardom, Warhol, influences, and related topics. Malanga, or whoever provided research for him, seems occasionally informed. Smith's responses are often hilarious. The clueless transcription runs a close second, as, for example:

> MAN: [Malanga] How have you managed not to be influenced by other new American cinema film makers?
> SMITH: By fasting. By continual prayer. By watching and waiting, and combined with self-immolation and the almost continuous study of science and health with keys to the scriptures by Mary Beckoretti.
> MAN: By whom?
> SMITH: By Mary Beckoretti. Combined with a strict diet of microbiotic rice.

Smith refers to his interest in the work of Mary Baker Eddy, founder of Christian Science. This interview is frequently referenced as one of a handful of important secondary sources by other writers, who may know it by tertiary reference or photocopy, as the journal's date and pagination are, occasionally, cited incorrectly. This issue of *Film Culture* also includes a coy interview with Mario Montez and "A Letter to An Unknown Woman Namely Jack Smith," by Warhol associate Robert Olivio (Ondine).

Niederkorn, William, et al. "The Artist Versus the Hippopotamus." *The True Comedy Planet* 1 – 3 (September 20, 1988, December 20, 1988, March 20, 1989), New York City: True Comedy Theatre Company, 1988, 1989. In this published transcript of the First True Comedy Symposium, August 15, 1988, the participants include Jack Smith and theater artists William Niederkorn and Jim Neu, and the painter, installation, and performance artist Ann Wilson. Founder of the True Comedy Theatre Company, Niederkorn cast Smith as Upton Sinclair in his *The Chaplin Acts*. This symposium took place before Smith left the *Acts* several days before its opening, although he appears in cast photos. Niederkorn refers to the machinery of commercial art as the "hippopotamus" of the transcript title. Smith talks about the importance of story-telling and baroque art, the poverty of American culture, the duplicity of critics and curators. In passing, Smith admires Veronese and Fragonard, and comments, in the second issue of the transcript, "What did I foster? An industry of drag queens? I'm ashamed of it."

—————. "Jack Smith: Excerpts from a Talking Performance." In "Pieces on Pieces," New York City: *Art-Rite* 6 (Summer, 1974): 19. This brief transcription from a lecture given by Smith at Artists Space painfully attempts to replicate the "oddities" of Smith's sometimes hesitant and mannered speech. Smith lectures on the irrationality of grant support for the arts, and describes his "last episode" with Mekas. *Art-Rite* was published and edited by Joshua Cohn, Walter Robinson, and Edit de Ak, and its roster of contributors, including Smith, is an impressive roel call of contemporary artists of many disciplines.

Drawings and related material by Jack Smith
provided courtesy of the Plaster Foundation, Inc.

Penguin Panic of the ~~Beach~~
Chiffon Jungle — can lead to
a penguin Stampede ~~of Rented Island~~
~~of~~ the Rented Desert —
Wait for me at the bottom of the Pool!!